I0813254

DEVOTIONS & PRAYERS FOR STRONG GIRLS

Renae Brumbaugh Green

DEVOTIONS & PRAYERS FOR STRONG GIRLS

Wisdom & Encouragement for Making a Difference

ISBN 979-8-89151-190-3

Published by Barbour Publishing, Inc., 1810 Barbour Drive, Uhrichsville, Ohio 44683, www.barbourbooks.com

Our mission is to inspire the world with the life-changing message of the Bible.

Printed in China.

002648 0925 DS

STRONG GIRL,
YOU CAN MAKE A DIFFERENCE!

Let no one show little respect for you because you are young. Show other Christians how to live by your life. They should be able to follow you in the way you talk and in what you do. Show them how to live in faith and in love and in holy living.

1 TIMOTHY 4:12

With every turn of the page, you'll discover that even though you're young, you can make a difference in the world. Each devotional reading will encourage you to embrace God's plan for your life, use your God-given gifts and abilities, and share the good news in your neighborhood, community, and beyond. You'll be challenged to make a positive change in the world around you as you rely on the heavenly Father for courage and strength. Turn the page and get ready to start a new adventure—as you become a courageous world changer!

CREATIVE GOD

Then the Lord God made man from the dust of the ground. And He breathed into his nose the breath of life. Man became a living being. . . . So the Lord God put the man to sleep as if he were dead. And while he was sleeping, He took one of the bones from his side and closed up the place with flesh. The Lord God made woman from the bone which He had taken from the man. And He brought her to the man.

GENESIS 2:7, 21–22

God took such care in making us! He scooped up some dust and formed Adam, then breathed His very own breath into his lungs. Then He put Adam to sleep and formed Eve from Adam's rib.

God is brilliantly creative, and we are His works of art. We are made in His image, which means He made us to be creative too. Whether we're working with clay, painting a picture, or helping prepare a meal, we honor God when we use our gifts and talents to create a loving environment for the people around us.

Dear Father, help me create a loving place for my family, friends, and others. Amen.

RIGHTEOUS

This is the story of Noah and his family. Noah was right with God. He was without blame in his time. Noah walked with God.

GENESIS 6:9

A person who is right with God is sometimes called "righteous." A righteous person tries to do the right thing and please God even when it's hard—even when no one is looking.

One reason Noah was right with God was because he spent time with Him. Today's verse from Genesis 6 tells us that Noah walked with God! He spent his days with God—talking to Him, listening to Him, and learning about His ways. The more time we spend with God, the more righteous we become.

Sometimes people made fun of Noah for doing the right thing and trying to please God. But God rewarded Noah for being righteous. People haven't changed much since Noah's time. Sometimes they still make fun of others for trying to live for God. It can be hard to do the right thing—but God *always* sees, and He will bless those who live to please Him.

Dear Father, I want to do the right thing and please You even when it's hard. Amen.

FOLLOW GOD

Dear friend, do not follow what is sinful, but follow what is good. The person who does what is good belongs to God. The person who does what is sinful has not seen God.

3 JOHN 11

This verse can be confusing at first. We *all* sin. Does that mean we don't belong to God?

The key to understanding this verse is the word *follow*. To follow something shows continued purpose. When we belong to God, His Spirit lives in us. We will mess up, but we will admit our mistakes and get right back to following God as soon as possible. Those who don't know God will follow after sin without giving it a second thought. They will continue to make choices that go against God's ways. Even if they seem sorry, they'll always go right back to their same old bad habits.

Without God's Holy Spirit in us, that's where we'd all be. God doesn't want His children to be overcome by sin and evil things. He wants us to stay focused on Him. He wants us to follow Him all our days.

Dear Father, I know Your ways are good.
I want to follow You all my life. Amen.

GOD IS IN HER

God is in the center of her. She will not be moved.
God will help her when the morning comes.

PSALM 46:5

This verse isn't talking about a girl. Instead, it refers to God's holy city and how God will protect the people in it. But it still makes sense, and sounds pretty cool, when we read it with ourselves in mind.

After all, God lives inside us. He lives in our hearts and gives us strength. Since our power and courage come from Him, we can be just as solid and steadfast as He is! Every minute of every day, God is right there, living and breathing within us. He's right there to help us when we need help.

Whenever you feel overwhelmed or afraid, remember this: "God is in the center of *you*. *You* will not be moved. God will help *you*."

Dear Father, thank You for this reminder that You live inside me. You give me strength and courage. You will never, ever leave me, and You're always there to help when I need it. With Your power, I know I can conquer anything. Amen.

SHOUTS AND WHISPERS

Then the woman said to the snake, "We may eat the fruit of the trees of the garden. But from the tree which is in the center of the garden, God has said, 'Do not eat from it or touch it, or you will die.'" The snake said to the woman, "No, you for sure will not die! For God knows that when you eat from it, your eyes will be opened and you will be like God, knowing good and bad."

GENESIS 3:2–5

Do you notice how Eve tried to do the right thing? She tried to resist temptation. But Satan doesn't give up easily. He tries to make us question ourselves and doubt what we know is right. He tries to make us think we're being silly. Satan likes to shout at us, in our thoughts, until we give in and do what he wants us to do. But God's Holy Spirit whispers what is right.

When you feel tempted to do something you know goes against God's ways, be still. Ask God to show you the right thing to do and to give you courage to do it.

Dear Father, help me ignore Satan's shouts so I can hear Your whispers. Amen.

NO MATTER WHAT

And the Lord God made clothes of skins for Adam and his wife, and dressed them.

GENESIS 3:21

Adam and Eve had messed up big-time. Eve listened to Satan and ate the fruit God told her not to eat. Then she talked Adam into doing the same thing. Because of what they did, they lost their innocence. They realized they were naked, and they were embarrassed for God to see them without clothes. Even though Adam and Eve disobeyed, God still loved them. He still took care of all their needs. Instead of getting mad at them for making a bad choice, God gave them clothes to wear.

We all goof up sometimes. But even when we make mistakes, we don't have to worry that God will stop loving us. When we come to Him and admit what we did, He holds out His arms and wraps us in His love. There is nothing we can do to make Him take away His love from us. And when our mistakes cause us to need His help, He's right there taking care of us, just like He always has.

Dear Father, thank You for loving me even when I mess up. Amen.

SAFE PLACE

After these things, the word of the Lord came to Abram in a special dream, saying, "Do not be afraid, Abram. I am your safe place. Your reward will be very great."

GENESIS 15:1

Right before this verse, Abram rescued his nephew, Lot, who had been captured. Even though Abram faced some pretty scary things, he kept doing what God told him to do. That's when God came to Abram in a dream and told him not to be afraid.

We face some pretty scary things today too. Whether it's a hard test in school or a mean person or an illness we don't understand, God is there. We can substitute in our own names: "Do not be afraid, (your name). I am your safe place." When we love God, live for Him, and make choices based on what will please Him, He notices. That's how Abram lived, and God rewarded him for it. He rewards us when we honor Him too.

Dear Father, thank You for being my safe place. I want to honor and obey You like Abram did. Amen.

NOTHING TOO HARD

"Is anything too hard for the Lord? I will return to you at this time next year, and Sarah will have a son."

GENESIS 18:14

Just before this verse, Sarah laughed at God for saying she'd have a baby. She thought she was too old to have children. People who have studied the Bible believe she was around ninety years old when Isaac was born! Most of us probably would have laughed too. But instead of getting angry with Sarah, God just asked her some questions: "Why did you laugh? Is anything too hard for the Lord?"

Sometimes when we face a really big problem, we might secretly think it's too big or too hard for God. But that's not true. Nothing is too hard for Him! Instead of worrying about things, we can simply ask ourselves the same question God asked of Sarah. "Is anything too hard for the Lord?" The answer will always be "No."

Dear Father, thank You for being so big and strong and powerful. I'm glad nothing is too hard for You. When I'm worried or afraid, remind me of this verse. Amen.

HUMILITY

But Jacob said, "No, I ask of you, if I have found favor in your eyes, then receive my gift. For I see your face as one sees the face of God. You have received me with favor. Take my gift that has been brought to you. For God has shown loving-kindness to me, and I have all I need." So he begged him until he took it.

GENESIS 33:10–11

Many years before this verse, Jacob had tricked his brother, Esau. He stole something precious from Esau. Then Jacob left, and the brothers hadn't seen each other in a long time. When Jacob returned, he sent expensive gifts ahead so Esau would know he was coming. The gifts softened Esau's heart. When the brothers finally saw each other, Esau was no longer angry. He tried to give the gifts back, but Jacob insisted Esau keep them. In this situation, Jacob showed humility.

When we have humility, we choose to treat others better than we treat ourselves. We admit when we've been wrong and ask others to forgive us.

Dear Father, teach me to have humility.
Help me treat others like they're important,
and help me admit when I'm wrong. Amen.

TAKING THE CREDIT

Pharaoh said to Joseph, "I have had a dream. But no one can tell me what it means. I have heard it said that you are able to hear a dream and tell what it means." Joseph answered Pharaoh, "Not by myself. God will give Pharaoh a good answer."

GENESIS 41:15–16

Joseph had a rough time. First his brothers sold him into slavery. Then his boss's wife set him up, and Joseph ended up in prison. Then he helped out some fellow prisoners, but they forgot all about Joseph when they were released. But after a long time, one of those prisoners told Pharaoh about Joseph. The pharaoh wanted Joseph to help him interpret a dream, but Joseph made sure Pharaoh knew it was God, not Joseph, who would provide answers. Joseph could have taken the credit for himself, but instead he gave God the credit.

Whenever we do something well, it's important to remind ourselves and others that God is the one who gave us our abilities, and God is the one who helps us succeed.

Dear Father, thank You for all the abilities You've given me. I want to give You the credit for every good thing I do. Amen.

HANG IN THERE

Two sons were born to Joseph before the years without food came. Asenath, the daughter of Potiphera, the religious leader of On, gave birth to them. Joseph gave the first-born the name Manasseh. "For," he said, "God has made me forget all my trouble and all those of my father's house." He gave the second son the name of Ephraim. "For," he said, "God has given me children in the land of my suffering."

GENESIS 41:50–52

Joseph went through many hard times. For years he probably thought nothing good would ever happen to him again. But time passed and God rewarded Joseph for his faithfulness. Joseph was given an important leadership position, and everyone except Pharaoh had to obey him. He got married and had two healthy sons. When the time of blessing finally came, Joseph kept honoring God and giving Him the credit. When hard times come, hang in there. They won't last forever. God sees your faithfulness, and blessings are coming your way.

Dear Father, sometimes I feel like giving up. When that happens, give me courage to keep going, and remind me that You have good things in store for my life. Amen.

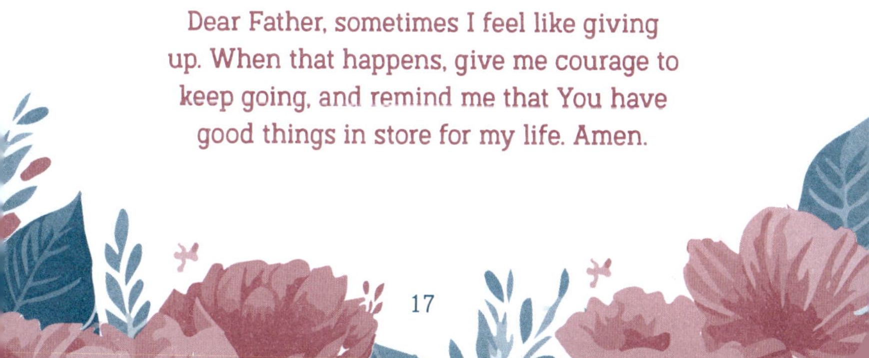

CHOOSE GOD

So God was good to the nurses. And the people became many and strong. Because the nurses feared God, He gave them families.

Exodus 1:20–21

During the time the Hebrews lived in Egypt, they grew in numbers. Pharaoh worried that there were too many Hebrews, so he asked the Hebrew nurses to do a really bad thing. He wanted them to make sure that when a Hebrew boy baby was born, he didn't live. That way those boys wouldn't grow to be strong men, and they couldn't build a powerful army. The Hebrew nurses knew it was more important to obey God than to obey an earthly king, so they ignored Pharaoh's command and took care of those boy babies. This made God happy, and He blessed the nurses.

Whenever we must choose between obeying God and obeying an earthly person, we must always choose God. The Bible tells us to respect our leaders and obey the law. But God is the most important. He will bless us for choosing Him.

Dear Father, please give us godly leaders so I don't have to choose between their laws and Your commands. If I ever must choose, give me courage to choose You. Amen.

TRUST AND OBEY

Moses and Aaron did what the Lord had told them. Aaron raised the special stick and hit the water of the Nile in front of Pharaoh and his servants. And all the water in the Nile was turned into blood.

Exodus 7:20

Moses was a Hebrew, but he was adopted by Pharaoh's daughter. Pharaoh treated Moses like he was family. Moses could talk to Pharaoh whenever he wanted, but the other Hebrews could not. God wanted Pharaoh to let the Hebrew people leave Egypt and become their own free nation again. But Pharaoh didn't want that, so he refused to let them go. To change Pharaoh's mind, God asked Moses and Aaron to do some pretty crazy things. If Moses had refused to obey God because he thought the command didn't make sense, Pharaoh wouldn't have seen how powerful God is.

When we know God is telling us to do something, He wants us to have faith, trust Him, and obey even when it doesn't make sense.

Dear Father, I want You to say about me what You said about Moses and Aaron: that I did everything You told me to do. Amen.

HARD-HEARTED

But when Pharaoh saw that there was rest from the trouble, he made his heart hard. He did not listen to them, just as the Lord had said.

Exodus 8:15

Moses did everything God told him to do, but Pharaoh still didn't change his mind. He wouldn't let the people go.

Some people are hard-hearted, which means they refuse to change in order to please God. When you meet someone who is hard-hearted, you may feel sad and discouraged. You may pray for them and wonder why your prayers aren't being answered. It's important to remember that God always has a plan. He can use even hard-hearted people to bring about His purpose. If you know a hard-hearted person, don't treat them unkindly. Continue to show God's love to them even when it's difficult. Keep praying. Keep caring about them. Then wait to see what great things God will do.

Dear Father, it's not easy to deal with hard-hearted people. Sometimes I don't understand why they won't listen to You. It feels like my prayers aren't working. Help me trust You even when others don't. I know You'll use everything that happens for good, to help bring about Your purpose. Amen.

HARD THINGS

Then the Lord said to Moses, "Pharaoh will not listen to you. So I will do more powerful works in the land of Egypt."

EXODUS 11:9

God kept asking Moses to talk to Pharaoh, but Pharaoh wouldn't listen. He was stubborn and hard-hearted. God sent miraculous signs so Pharaoh would believe, but those signs only made Pharaoh angry. Moses was probably afraid each time he approached Pharaoh. After all, Pharaoh was the king, and he could throw Moses in prison or worse! Why wouldn't God just change Pharaoh's heart?

Sometimes God allows us to go through difficult things so He can show His power. If Pharaoh had let the Hebrews go easily, a lot of people might have missed seeing God's miracles. And if our lives were always easy, the people around us might miss seeing the amazing ways God works in our lives. When we go through difficult things, we can trust that God has a plan. He will accomplish His purpose, and the end will be good.

Dear Father, going through hard things isn't fun. But I know it's through the hard things in my life that You shine. I trust Your love for me even in difficult times. Amen.

CHANGE OF HEART

The people of Israel had done what Moses had said. They had asked the Egyptians for things made of silver and gold and for clothes. And the Lord had given the people favor in the eyes of the Egyptians. So the Egyptians let them have whatever they asked for. And they took the best things of Egypt.

Exodus 12:35–36

The Hebrew people, also known as the Israelites, were slaves to the Egyptians. The Egyptians didn't want the Israelites to leave—they'd lose all their servants. Who would do the work? Even though the Egyptians didn't want the Israelites to leave, God worked in their hearts. He caused them to give all sorts of valuable things to the Hebrews so they'd have plenty for their journey.

When we stay close to God, God can make even those who don't like us be nice to us. He can cause them to want good things for us.

Dear Father, I don't like it when people are mean to me. Help me to treat them with kindness and love anyway. Please change their hearts and make them want to be nice to me. Amen.

GET YOUR POPCORN READY

"The Lord will fight for you. All you have to do is keep still."

Exodus 14:14

Do you like to watch movies or plays? Sometimes it's fun to eat popcorn while we're watching a story play out in front of us.

When we're going through hard times, it helps to remember that God is the author of our lives. He doesn't want our story to be boring, so He allows some hard things to happen. Those hard things are what make our stories interesting! When troubles come, we don't have to fight on our own. God likes to show His power, so He will fight for us. All He asks is that we stay calm, trust Him, and watch the great things He will do.

Next time you face a battle in your life, remember to remain calm. Stay still and let God work. Get your popcorn ready, because He's about to do something great.

Dear Father, thank You for fighting for me. When troubles come, remind me to be still and trust You. I can't wait to see the great things You'll do in my life. Amen.

WATER WALL

And when the morning came, the Egyptians ran into the wall of water as the sea returned to the way it was before. The Lord destroyed the Egyptians in the sea.

EXODUS 14:27

After many signs and miracles from God, Pharaoh finally allowed the Israelites to leave. But after they left, he changed his mind again. He and his army set out to follow them and bring them back into slavery. The Israelites were frightened! They had the sea in front of them and the army behind them. How could they escape? God parted that sea right down the middle, and the Israelites crossed through like it was a highway. Pharaoh's army followed them, but once the Israelites were on the other side, God caused the wall of water to crash back down on top of the army.

Never, ever forget how powerful God is. No matter what problem we face, God is bigger. All He expects us to do is trust Him, obey Him, and be patient. He will do amazing things. He still works miracles!

Dear Father, when things get scary and I feel like there's no way to escape, remind me of how powerful You are. I trust You. Amen.

OBEY GOD

[The Lord] said, "Listen well to the voice of the Lord your God. Do what is right in His eyes. Listen to what He tells you, and obey all His Laws. If you do this, I will put none of the diseases on you which I have put on the Egyptians. For I am the Lord Who heals you."

Exodus 15:26

When we follow God's laws, we still feel the effects of sin. But we are less likely to suffer the consequences of sin when we obey and stay close to Him. His laws are designed to protect us. His rules are not there to keep us from having fun. Instead, He has given us guidelines to keep us safe from harm.

Think of it this way: If we wash our hands and take our vitamins, we still might catch a cold. But if we don't do those things, and we eat from the same dish or drink from the same cup of our friend who has a cold, we're a whole lot more likely to get a cold than if we take precautions. Obeying God doesn't mean bad things will never happen, but obedience does bring protection.

Dear Father, I trust You. Help me obey You. Amen.

DON'T DO IT ALONE

"You and the people with you will become tired and weak. For the work is too much for you. You cannot do it alone."

Exodus 18:18

Moses was the leader of the Israelites. There were a lot of them, and they were way out in the desert. They were tired and hungry. They had many complaints, and Moses tried to listen to everyone and help solve all the problems. Moses' father-in-law saw what was happening and knew it was too big a job for just one man. He told Moses to find some helpers so Moses wouldn't have to do it alone.

It's important to have godly friends and family around so we can have help when we need it. It's also important to offer help when others need it. God likes it when we work together and help each other out. He didn't create us to be alone.

Dear Father, thank You for friends and family. Show me when others need help and how I can assist them. When I'm overwhelmed, help me accept help from others. Amen.

IF

"Now then, if you will obey My voice and keep My agreement, you will belong to Me from among all nations. For all the earth is Mine."

EXODUS 19:5

The word *if* is such a small word, but it holds a lot of power. It means there is a condition to God's promise. If we obey Him, and if we keep up our end of the agreement to honor and serve Him only, we will belong to Him.

Imagine that! We are children of the Most High God, the King of kings and Lord of lords. Everything in the earth belongs to Him, and so do we. He will love us and protect us as His treasured possessions.

Not everyone belongs to God, though. Only those who understand the "if" statements, only those who agree to and obey the conditions, are covered by His promises. God wants everyone to belong to Him. More than anything, He wants everyone to be His daughters and sons. But He won't force anyone. He gives us a choice. Have you made the choice to follow Him?

Dear Father, thank You for Your promises to me. I choose You. Amen.

I WILL OBEY

Then he took the Book of the Agreement and read it for the people to hear. They said, "We will do all that the Lord has spoken. We will obey."

EXODUS 24:7

God had a private meeting with Moses. He explained all the important things He required of the Israelites. After this meeting, Moses told the people everything God had said. He clearly explained the rules they needed to follow. The people agreed. Then, to make sure they didn't forget, Moses wrote down all the words God had spoken and read them out loud to the people. Once again the people agreed to do everything God told them to do.

Today we have God's written Word, the Bible. It tells us all the things God said and the things He wants us to do. It is our job to do as the Israelites did. We must listen to and read God's Word and obey Him.

Dear Father, thank You for giving me the Bible so I can read and understand the things You said. Thank You for Your laws—I know they are designed to protect me. I want to obey everything You've told me to do. Amen.

SKILLS AND TALENTS

"Make holy clothing for your brother Aaron, for honor and for beauty. Tell all the able workmen, whom I have given the spirit of wisdom, to make Aaron's clothing to set him apart for My work. He will work for Me as a religious leader."

EXODUS 28:2–3

Do you enjoy wearing pretty clothes? God is a creative God, and He enjoys beautiful things. He commanded his most skilled tailors—people who make clothing—to create something really special for the religious leader Aaron. God gives everyone special gifts and talents to use for Him. He expects us to develop those talents the best we can. He wants us to use them to share His love with others and point people to Him.

The people in this passage could sew—they had spent years learning to sew well. Some people cook delicious meals. Some paint beautiful pictures. Some are athletes. Some use their skills to instruct or entertain. Whatever skills God has given you, use them! Practice, and become the best you can be. Then use what you have to glorify God.

Dear Father, help me develop the skills and talents You've given me so I can use them for You. Amen.

LIVE AMONG THEM

"I will live among the people of Israel and will be their God. They will know that I am the Lord their God, Who brought them out of the land of Egypt to live among them. I am the Lord their God."

EXODUS 29:45–46

Does everyone around you know God? Probably not. But God desires for everyone to know Him. When we know God, He lives inside us. And when we go to school or to the grocery store or to play with the kids on our street, God lives among those people. He lives there because *you* are there, and He lives in *you*!

When you find yourself around people who don't know God, think of this verse, and use it as a prayer. Ask God to live among the people at your school or in your town. Ask that they will come to know Him and make Him their God. And ask Him to make His presence so obvious in your life that others will want what you have.

Dear Father, please live among the people
of (your town) and be their God.
Let them know that You are Lord. Amen.

POWERFUL PRAYERS

The Lord said to Moses, "I will do what you have said. For you have found favor in My eyes, and I have known you by name."

EXODUS 33:17

Moses went away from the people of Israel so he could talk to God alone. He stayed gone a long time. When he didn't come back quickly, the Israelites got impatient. They thought God had abandoned them, so they made a golden calf and worshipped it. When Moses came back and saw what had happened, he was upset. But God was furious! God was so angry, He told Moses to take the people and go. God would not go with them because He was too upset.

Moses asked God to forgive the people. He begged God to stay with them. Finally, God agreed. Because God loved Moses and He knew Moses loved Him, He did what Moses asked. When we love God and obey Him, our prayers are powerful. When we live to honor God, He wants to bless us and do what we ask.

Dear Father, I want to honor You the way Moses did. More than anything, I want my life to please You.

FOLLOWING INSTRUCTIONS

Bezalel, the son of Uri, son of Hur, of the family of Judah, made all that the Lord had told Moses.

Exodus 38:22

When the Israelites built the things used in worship, God had specific instructions for each item. Whether it was a table or a bowl or the clothes worn by the priests, God told exactly how He wanted each item made. When all was completed, God was impressed with Bezalel. He wanted to make sure everyone knew about Bezalel and the work he did. It is recorded this way so everyone would remember him.

God has given each of us specific tasks to do for Him. As you obey God and follow His instructions, imagine Him saying, "(Your name), daughter of (your parents' names), family of (your last name), did everything I asked her to do." Even if our names are never recorded that way, it should be our goal to do everything God wants us to do.

Dear Father, thank You for Bezalel's example. He followed Your instructions and made everything just as You commanded. I want You to say the same of me. Help me understand and obey Your instructions for my life. Amen.

WELL DONE

So the people of Israel did all the work just as the Lord had told Moses.

Exodus 39:42

A lot of work needed to be done to get everything ready for God's place of worship. When the people finished, it was time for inspection. Moses looked at everything and examined each item closely. If anyone had taken shortcuts or not done their best work, Moses would have noticed. He wanted to make sure they followed all God's instructions. The Israelites may have been nervous as they waited to hear what Moses thought of their work. Finally, Moses told them it all passed inspection! He may have smiled and said, "Good job."

Our goal should be that when we reach the end of our time here on earth, God will inspect all the things we did for Him and say, "Good job."

Dear Father, You gave the Israelites a lot of work to do and specific instructions for how to do it. I know You've planned many special tasks for my life as well. I want to obey You in everything I do for the rest of my life. When I complete my work here, I want You to say, "Well done." Amen.

FRAGRANT PRAYERS

"Then Aaron's sons will burn [the offering] on the altar, on the burnt gift that is on the wood of the fire. It is a gift by fire, a pleasing smell to the Lord."

LEVITICUS 3:5

Do you ever smell something delicious coming from the kitchen and your stomach starts to growl? Maybe someone is baking cookies and your mouth waters. You think, *I love it when Dad bakes cookies.* Delicious smells are one of God's favorite things.

In this verse, the priests offered a food offering, and it smelled wonderful. In the book of Revelation, we're told that our prayers are incense to God. Incense is a pleasant fragrance. When we pray, God breathes in our prayers and says, "Oh, I love it when My children talk to Me." God is a sensory God, and He loves things that smell good. Our prayers bring Him pleasure, and He wants us to talk to Him all the time!

Dear Father, thank You for telling me my prayers are like a wonderful fragrance to You. This helps me understand that I can talk to You anytime about anything and You will listen. Remind me to talk to You all through the day. Amen.

PAYING THE PRICE

"Say to the people of Israel, 'If a person sins without meaning to, by not obeying what the Lord has told us to do, these are the rules he must follow. If the chosen religious leader sins and so brings guilt on the people, let him give to the Lord a bull that is perfect. It is a sin gift for the sin he has done.'"

LEVITICUS 4:2–3

Have you ever done the wrong thing without meaning to? Maybe you were trying to do the right thing at the time, but looking back, you realize you should have made a different choice. When we sin without meaning to, it's still sin. In the Old Testament, people paid for their sins by offering an animal. They had to give these offerings quite often because they kept sinning.

When Jesus died for our sins, He died for *all* our sins. He died for the accidental sins and the on-purpose sins, the sins we've done and the sins we will do in the future. Our entire lives should be lived as a thank-you to Christ for doing away with our sins.

Dear Jesus, thank You for paying the price for my sins. I love You. Amen.

WHEN SOMEONE HURTS US

"Do not hurt someone who has hurt you. Do not keep on hating the sons of your people, but love your neighbor as yourself. I am the Lord."

LEVITICUS 19:18

When someone hurts us or is unkind, it's only natural to want to hurt them back. But if we do that, they'll just be mean to us again, and the cycle will continue. When we set our hearts on hurting others who have hurt us, it causes us to be angry and sad and stuck in a bad mood.

God wants better for us. He wants us to let Him take care of things when others hurt us. He doesn't want us to waste our lives being upset. Instead, He wants us to focus on Him and His love. He wants us to love others the way we love ourselves. We wouldn't purposely hurt ourselves, so why would we do that to others? God sees every hurt we endure, and He will take care of it in His time. Let Him handle things. Focus on love, and you'll live a much happier life.

Dear Father, when someone hurts me,
give me wisdom to know how to respond. Amen.

WORK!

They were each given their work and load to carry,
as the Lord told them to do through Moses. So these were
his numbered men, just as the Lord had told Moses.

NUMBERS 4:49

Have you ever tried to do a really big job, like clean a messy kitchen, all by yourself? When you work alone, it takes a long time. The person doing the work might get grumpy because she's having to do everything without help. But if everyone does their part, the work goes much faster.

In this passage, God gave each group of people specific work to do. Everyone did their part, and God was pleased. The Lord has given each of us specific work to do as well. He doesn't expect us to do it all, but we each must do our part. When we all do the tasks we've been assigned, the work is easier and more effective. What work has God given you?

Dear Father, show me the work You want me to do.
Help me do it to the best of my ability. Amen.

BLESSING OTHERS

"May the Lord bring good to you and keep you. May the Lord make His face shine upon you, and be kind to you. May the Lord show favor toward you, and give you peace."

NUMBERS 6:24–26

God told Moses to say these words to Aaron and his sons. Aaron's family was in charge of the spiritual guidance of Israel. They were the priests, or ministers.

God wants the people in ministry to have special blessings, and He wants the rest of us to have a part in those blessings. We should love, care for, and pray for the people God has called to lead our churches. He also wants us to make a habit of blessing, or bringing good things to, the people around us even if they're not in the ministry. When we show kindness, we imitate God, and He is pleased. God loves to bless people, and He wants us to bless others too.

Dear Father, help me bless someone today. Show me ways to offer kindness, love, and encouragement to those around me. Remind me to pray special prayers for the people in ministry. Amen.

TIME WITH GOD

Moses went into the meeting tent to speak with the Lord. And he heard the voice speaking to him from above the mercy-seat that was on the special box with the Law, between the two cherubim. So the Lord spoke to him.

NUMBERS 7:89

Moses made a habit of talking to God often. We can talk to God anywhere, anytime. But in this case, Moses had a special place He wanted to meet with God. It was a holy place. By going there, Moses was certain he wouldn't be disturbed. He heard God speaking to him.

God still speaks to us today. When we make time with God a priority and set aside a specific time and place to meet with Him, He will often speak to us! It probably won't be an out-loud voice. Most often we hear His voice clearly in our thoughts, and we know it's Him. Do you have a special place where you like to meet with God? If not, think about setting aside a time and place to talk to and listen to God.

Dear Father, thank You for letting me talk to You anytime. Time with You is important to me. Amen.

THE CLOUD

The people of Israel would move on as the Lord told them. And they would set up their tents as the Lord told them. They stayed in one place as long as the cloud rested over the meeting tent. Even when the cloud rested over the meeting tent for many days, the people of Israel would obey the Lord and not leave.

NUMBERS 9:18–19

When the Israelites wandered in the desert, God set up a special sign for them. If a particular cloud rested over their place of worship, they stayed put. If the cloud moved, they packed up everything and followed. The cloud served many purposes. It hid them from enemies and kept them safe. It reminded them of the importance of obeying God and waiting on Him.

Those are important lessons for us today. When we're not sure what to do, we should stay still and wait on God to direct us. He may be protecting us from something we don't know about, or He may be preparing us for something in the future.

Dear Father, show me Your wisdom like You showed the Israelites that cloud. If I'm not sure what to do, remind me to wait until You make it clear. Amen.

A MAN WITH NO PRIDE

Now Moses was a man with no pride,
more so than any man on the earth.
NUMBERS 12:3

When the Bible says Moses didn't have any pride, it means he was meek and humble. He had been brought up in Pharaoh's palace with all the riches he could want. He was more educated than the Israelites around him. It would have been easy for him to think he was smarter or better than others, but he didn't.

The word *meek* means humble, patient, and quiet. It can also mean gentle and kind. Moses was special to God because of his humble and gentle nature. God loves everyone, and He doesn't like it when we think we're better than someone else. It's important to treat others with humility, gentleness, and kindness. When we set aside our pride and treat others like they're the important ones, God is pleased.

Dear Father, sometimes I struggle with pride, thinking I'm more important than others. Teach me to be humble like Moses. Help me to treat others with patience and kindness. Amen.

A DIFFERENT SPIRIT

"But My servant Caleb has had a different spirit and has followed Me in every way. I will bring him into the land where he went, and his children will take it for themselves."

NUMBERS 14:24

When the Israelites wandered in the desert those forty years, many people got tired and impatient. They grumbled against God for not making it easy for them. They got upset and refused to obey God. But God forgave them and took care of them anyway. Still, God noticed Caleb because he didn't act like everyone else. He loved and obeyed God. He was humble. Instead of grumbling, he thanked God for caring for them. As a reward for Caleb's attitude, God made sure that Caleb and his family made it into the Promised Land.

When everyone around us has a bad attitude, it's easy to get pulled in. But God notices when we don't act like the crowd. He is pleased when we honor and obey Him even if no one else does.

Dear Father, I want to be like Caleb.
I want to honor You with my words and actions
even when no one else does. Amen.

OBEY GOD NO MATTER WHAT

Balaam answered, "Must I not be careful to speak what the Lord puts in my mouth?"

NUMBERS 23:12

Balak was the king of Moab, and Balaam was a sorcerer, a person who does magic. Balak was afraid the Israelites were growing too powerful, and he was fearful of what they might do. He sent for Balaam and asked him to curse the Israelites. (To curse people is to try to make bad things happen to them.) Balak said he would pay Balaam a lot of riches to do this. But God spoke to Balaam and told him not to curse the Israelites. Balaam was smart to listen to God. He knew God was more powerful than any magic. He told Balak no and turned down all the riches.

No matter what the world tries to offer us, it's always better to obey God.

Dear Father, sometimes I'm tempted to do the wrong thing because I want people to like me. But I know that even if I make others angry by obeying You, it's more important to obey You. Amen.

COURAGE TO DO WHAT'S RIGHT

But Balaam answered Balak, "Did I not tell you that I must do whatever the Lord says?"

NUMBERS 23:26

Balak kept trying to convince Balaam to curse the Israelites. He took Balaam to another place, thinking it might be easier to curse them if he couldn't see them as well. Balaam went with Balak, but he still listened to God. God told him, "Don't curse the Israelites. Instead, I want you to bless them." So Balaam spoke a blessing over Israel. Balak was upset that Balaam wouldn't do what he wanted.

Sometimes people try very hard to convince us to do what they want us to do. If they're doing something God doesn't like, they feel better if someone goes along with them. But God doesn't ever want us to curse people or be mean to them! He calls us to love others, show kindness, and do the right thing. He wants us to bless people and show His love to the world.

Dear Father, when others try to convince me to be unkind, remind me that Your opinion of me is more important than theirs. Give me courage to bless others and obey You no matter what. Amen.

DOING THE RIGHT THING

These are the men whom the Lord told to divide the land among the people of Israel in the land of Canaan.

NUMBERS 34:29

When it was time to divide the land among the tribes of Israel, God chose men He could trust, men He knew would do the right thing. It would have been easy for people to try to get the best land for themselves or try to get more land for their families. God needed people in charge who had good character and would do the right thing no matter what.

Still today, God needs trustworthy people to do His work. He looks for people who obey Him and do the right thing even when no one is looking. When we show God we love Him and want to please Him even when it's hard, He notices. If we want God to bless us with important jobs, we must show Him that we're trustworthy.

Dear Father, I hope You can trust me to do the right thing no matter what. Help me obey You even when it's hard. Amen.

ALWAYS GOOD

"For the Lord your God has brought good to you in all you have done. He knows about your traveling through this big desert. The Lord your God has been with you these forty years. You have not been without a thing."

DEUTERONOMY 2:7

The Israelites wandered around the desert for forty years, waiting to find the land God had promised them. They didn't like traveling for that long. Each time they moved, they had to pack everything up and carry it with them. They didn't always know what kind of food they'd have, and they had to trust God to provide. Many of the Israelites grumbled and complained because life was so hard. But God never stopped caring for His people even when they were ungrateful. He brought them food to eat and water to drink. He protected them from all kinds of weather and bad events.

God is love, and there is nothing unkind in Him. When you aren't happy with your life or you feel God isn't taking care of you, it helps to stop and think about all the good things He has done.

Dear Father, thank You for always being good to me. Amen.

DON'T BE AFRAID

"Do not be afraid of them. For the Lord your God is the One fighting for you."

DEUTERONOMY 3:22

Moses had been Israel's leader for a long time. Now he was old, and it was time to appoint the next leader. He knew Joshua was the man God had chosen. Moses wanted to encourage Joshua, because he knew Joshua would face some scary things. "Don't be afraid," he told Joshua. "God is fighting for you."

That is true for each of us. When we have God living inside us, we have nothing to fear. As long as we listen to and obey God, we can know He is fighting for us. In 1 John 4:4, we are told, "The One Who lives in you is stronger than the one who is in the world." We all face hard things in our lives. Sometimes we'll face things that scare us. When that happens, remember the words Moses spoke to Joshua: "Don't be afraid. God is fighting for you."

Dear Father, thank You for living in me and fighting for me. When I feel afraid, remind me of Your power. Amen.

BE CAREFUL!

"Only be careful. Keep watch over your life. Or you might forget the things you have seen. Do not let them leave your heart for the rest of your life. But teach them to your children and to your grandchildren."

DEUTERONOMY 4:9

Moses knew he would die soon, and he wanted to pass on as much wisdom as he could to the Israelites. He'd spent much of his life leading them, and he wanted to make sure they'd keep following God after he was gone. He told them to keep a careful watch over their lives. He knew life would bring many things to distract them from their one true purpose: to love God and serve Him only.

That advice, given to the Israelites so long ago, applies to us today. We must carefully watch over our lives. We must not allow ourselves to forget how powerful and wonderful God is. We mustn't allow ourselves to be distracted from our purpose: to love God and serve Him only.

Dear Father, help me be careful with how I spend my time and attention. I want to live out Your purpose for my life. Amen.

IF ONLY

"If only they had such a heart in them that they would fear Me and live by all My Laws always! Then it would go well with them and with their children forever."

DEUTERONOMY 5:29

The people of Israel did some really bad things and broke God's laws. But when they realized what they had done, they admitted they were wrong and asked God to forgive them. They were ashamed and sorry for their actions. Because they knew how powerful God is, they were afraid of how He would react. God responded with the words in this verse. "If only they always cared so much! If only they always honored and respected Me. If only. . .then their lives would be so much better."

The same is true for us today. The more we honor God and obey His Word, the better our lives. We will still face hard things, but overall things are smoother, more peaceful, and more pleasant when we live according to His Word.

Dear Father, I want my heart to belong to You completely all the time. Help me honor You with my life. Amen.

BECAUSE HE IS LOVE

"Understand that it is not because you are right with God that the Lord your God is giving you this good land for your own, for you are a strong-willed people. Remember and do not forget how you made the Lord your God angry in the desert. You have gone against the Lord from the day you left the land of Egypt until you came to this place."

DEUTERONOMY 9:6–7

When God blesses us, it's easy to become prideful and think it's because we're good. But Isaiah 64:6 tells us that our very best is like filthy rags to God. There's nothing we can do to earn His love or His blessings. Even when we try our hardest, we can't compare to God's goodness. He blesses us because He is good, not because *we* are good. We should honor and obey Him out of sincere thanks. He is pleased when we try to honor Him. But He pours out His love on us because He is love and it is His nature to love.

Dear Father, thank You for loving me and blessing me in so many ways. I want my life to be a long thank-you letter to You. Amen.

SECOND CHANCES

"At that time the Lord said to me, 'Cut out for yourself two pieces of stone like the other ones. Then come up to Me on the mountain, and make a box of wood. I will write on the pieces of stone the words that were on the other pieces of stone which you broke. And you will put them in the box.'"

DEUTERONOMY 10:1–2

Did you know God gives second chances? Moses broke the first set of commandments when he got angry at the Israelites. So God told him to get two more pieces of stone and meet Him on the mountain. God wrote the entire list of commandments again.

It's important to remember that God gives us second chances. When we make mistakes, Satan wants us to think we've blown it for good. But as long as we're sorry for our sins, God always wants to help us make a new start. We often have to live with the results of our poor choices, but past failures do not define our future. Whenever you think you've messed up too much, ask God to help you start fresh.

Dear Father, thank You for being the God of second chances. Amen.

INSTRUCTION GUIDE

"Be careful to listen to all these words I am telling you. Then it will go well with you and your children after you forever. For you will be doing what is good and right in the eyes of the Lord your God."

DEUTERONOMY 12:28

The Bible is an instruction book for life. It offers wisdom for all kinds of things. When we study God's Word, it's like we're spending time in His classroom. He teaches us how to live the best life possible. Many people have Bibles in their homes, but they rarely read the words written inside. Then they wonder why they make poor choices and why their lives and their relationships aren't what they'd hoped for. Reading God's Word doesn't ensure that we'll get everything we want. Instead, it helps us view life differently. It helps us be humbler, more thankful, and more compassionate to others. These traits help us live happier, more joyful lives.

Dear Father, thank You for Your Word, which is my instruction guide for life. Help me make reading my Bible and spending time with You a priority.

PICK ME!

"For you are a holy nation to the Lord your God. The Lord has chosen you to be His own nation out of all the nations on the earth."

DEUTERONOMY 14:2

Have you ever wanted to be chosen for something? Maybe you wanted to be picked for a certain sports team or club. Or maybe you wanted to be included in a certain group of friends. Most of us have had that struggle. We want something, but it's dependent on someone else choosing us for that thing. We may act like we don't care, but secretly we're all whispering, "Pick me! Pick me!"

There's good news. God Himself, the King of kings and Lord over all creation, has already chosen you! He thought you up. He designed every part of you because He thought you were a good idea. And as long as you have breath in your body, He will choose you. Just as He chose Israel to be His special nation, He chose you to be His special child.

Dear Father, thank You for choosing me. Thank You for making me Your child and making me feel special and loved. Amen.

GIVING LIKE GOD

"Give much to him, without being sorry that you do. Because the Lord your God will bring good to you for this, in all your work and in everything you do. The poor will always be in the land. So I tell you to be free in giving to your brother, to those in need, and to the poor in your land."

DEUTERONOMY 15:10–11

God made us in His image. That means He made us to be like Him. One of His favorite things is to bless us. If we're supposed to be like Him, that means we should bless others. God likes to bless us with things we can't do for ourselves. So when we see someone who needs help, we should bless them. God is generous with us, so we should be generous with others.

We might be tempted to give only things we don't want for ourselves. But the real blessing comes when we give abundantly. When we give generously to others, we find a personal joy in living out our purpose to be like God.

Dear Father, teach me to give generously to others the way You give to me. Amen.

GIVING BACK

"Every man should give as he is able, as the Lord your God has given to you."
DEUTERONOMY 16:17

God gives us so much, and He wants us to give back to Him. Whether we give our time, our money, or our talent, it's important to give to God. He says we should each give as we are able. The amount we give may not be the same for everyone, but God isn't concerned about that. He simply wants us to take what we have and give it back to Him.

If you don't have much money but you have a lot of time, you might give to God by helping an elderly neighbor. You could take out the trash, sweep the floor, or mow the lawn for that person. If you don't have much time or money but you're really good at basketball, maybe you could spend a few minutes each day helping your younger brother develop his skills. When we give generously of what we have, we imitate God and He is pleased.

Dear Father, show me what You want me to give back to You. I want to be generous like You. Amen.

EVERY SINGLE DAY

"[This Law] should be kept with [the king] and he should read it all the days of his life. Then he will learn to fear the Lord his God, by being careful to obey all the words of these Laws."

DEUTERONOMY 17:19

God made certain laws specifically for the kings of Israel. One law was that each king would write out his own copy of God's Word (see Deuteronomy 17:18). Then he had to read it every single day. This shows the importance of reading the Bible every day. God's Word contains wisdom for everything in life. God commanded the kings of Israel to study it each day so they would be wise rulers.

If His Word is that powerful, why wouldn't we all spend time each day reading it, thinking about it, and absorbing it into our minds? Remember, as children of God, we are royalty. God has called each of us to fulfill a specific purpose. His Word teaches us how to make good decisions, how to treat other people, and how to live the best possible life.

Dear Father, thank You for giving us Your Word. Help me make reading it and thinking about what it says a priority. Amen.

KEEP AWAY

"When you go as an army against those who hate you, keep yourself away from every sinful thing."

DEUTERONOMY 23:9

God warned the people of Israel that they would have enemies who wanted to hurt them. When they faced those enemies, it was important to have God's power behind them.

The best way to experience God's power in our lives is to keep ourselves pure. We do this by staying close to God and staying far away from sin and evil. Sin destroys us. It weakens us. Satan wants us to sin because he knows it will demolish our lives and diminish our power as God's children. When you face people who are unkind, who are mean and want to hurt you, don't give in to the temptation to become like them. Stay close to God and keep yourself pure from sin. His power in your life will protect you and make you strong.

Dear Father, I know sin destroys me. Forgive me for the times I've messed up. Thank You for making me pure through Jesus Christ. Help me stay close to You and far away from sin. Amen.

TREASURED

"And the Lord today has made it known that you are His own people, as He promised you, and that you should keep all His Laws."

DEUTERONOMY 26:18

God has made it known that we're His people. He's proud that we belong to Him, and He doesn't want to keep it a secret. Another translation of the Bible says He declared that we are His treasured possession. Isn't that amazing?

A treasure is something of great value. To say that we're God's treasured possession means that He values us more than anything else. Think about that. The God of the universe, the Creator of all things, the King of kings and Lord of lords values us more than all His other possessions. He owns it all, and He cherishes us above everything. Because we hold such a special place in His heart, it's important that we keep His laws and live for Him. That's how we show our gratitude to God for loving us so much.

Dear Father, I'm overwhelmed by Your love for me. Thank You for loving me and making me Your treasured child. Amen.

LIVE FOR JESUS

"Be faithful in obeying the Lord your God. Be careful to keep all His Laws which I tell you today. And the Lord your God will set you high above all the nations of the earth."

DEUTERONOMY 28:1

God loves to bless His children. He wants to bless us so much, He told us exactly what we need to do to be blessed. In essence He said, "If you obey Me and honor My laws, I will bless you more than anyone else on earth."

When we accept Christ as Savior and live our lives for Him, we will end up with the greatest blessing of all: living in heaven with Jesus forever. But even here on earth we receive amazing gifts from God. When we honor Him in the way we treat others, we have better relationships. When we stay away from sin, we avoid all kinds of bad consequences. When we use our time, money, and talents for Him, we gain a satisfaction with life that many never experience. Live for Him, and you'll live the best life you can imagine.

Dear Father, thank You for Your promises.
I want to live for You every single day. Amen.

DAY AND NIGHT

"This book of the Law must not leave your mouth. Think about it day and night, so you may be careful to do all that is written in it. Then all will go well with you. You will receive many good things."

JOSHUA 1:8

God's Word teaches us everything we need to know to live a peaceful, successful life. It's important to know that God's definition of success isn't the same as the world's definition of success. Some people may not live for God or honor His laws, and they still may become wealthy or successful in the world's eyes. But real peace, real joy, real contentment can only be found through a close relationship with God.

When we spend time in God's Word, we spend time with God. Reading His Word is like listening to Him talk to us, and praying is talking to Him. The more time we spend with God, the more we know Him, and the more He blesses us with those gifts that come only from God. Do you spend time reading and thinking about God's Word each day?

Dear Father, I want to spend time with You every day. Thank You for loving me so much. Amen.

BE STRONG

"Have I not told you? Be strong and have strength of heart! Do not be afraid or lose faith. For the Lord your God is with you anywhere you go."

JOSHUA 1:9

Moses was Israel's leader for a long time. When Moses died, Joshua became the leader. He was much younger than Moses, and leading a nation was a big responsibility! He was probably nervous. He may have worried that he wouldn't do a good job. But God told him not to be afraid! Instead, he was to be strong and have faith. God promised to stay with Joshua through everything.

Do you feel nervous or afraid about something? Remember God's words to Joshua. Be strong and courageous! Hold on to your faith in God. He is with you wherever you go, and He will never, ever leave you.

Dear Father, a lot of things make me feel anxious and afraid. Sometimes I worry about new situations and people. Other times I'm afraid I'll fail or that something bad will happen. Thank You for Your promise never to leave me. Help me to be strong and courageous and to rely on You. Amen.

JUST OBEY

Then Joshua told the leaders of the people, "Go among the tents and tell the people, 'Gather together the things you will need. For within three days you will cross this Jordan to go in to take the land the Lord your God is giving you for your own.'"

JOSHUA 1:10–11

Look carefully at these verses. Did God tell the people to get ready to fight? Did He ask them to gather their weapons? He did not. He told them, "Get your stuff together. You're about to arrive at your new home." God *gave* them the land. All they had to do was obey Him.

All God ever requires is our obedience. We don't need to be successful by the world's standards. We don't even need to be particularly capable or smart or talented. All God wants is our pure-hearted obedience. When we follow God and are careful to do all He asks us to do, He will take care of all our needs.

Dear Father, thank You for this reminder that all You really want from me is obedience. Help me to always listen to You and obey Your voice. Amen.

THE COMPARISON TRAP

When Saul saw and knew that the Lord was with David and that his daughter Michal loved him, Saul was even more afraid of David. So he hated David always.

1 SAMUEL 18:28–29

God chose Saul to be king of Israel. Saul had God's blessings. He had nothing to worry about with David. But when he saw how much everyone loved David, Saul became jealous. He worried that people would love David more than they loved Saul. Even Saul's daughter was in love with David! This made Saul so angry he wanted to kill David—which was sad because David loved Saul and never would have done anything to hurt him.

Because God blesses each of us in different ways, we should never compare ourselves to others. We should spend our time being grateful for the ways God has blessed us instead of angry that He blessed someone else in a different way. Next time you're tempted to compare yourself to someone else, shift your focus. Think about the person God created *you* to be, and be grateful for all He's given *you*.

Dear Father, forgive me for comparing myself to others. Thank You for all You've given me. Amen.

GODLY PEOPLE

Now David ran away from Saul and came to Samuel at Ramah. He told him all that Saul had done to him. Then he and Samuel went and stayed in Naioth.

1 SAMUEL 19:18

Saul was the king, and he was angry with David. Though David hadn't done anything wrong, he was afraid of Saul and his army. David knew Saul was trying to kill him. When he was afraid, he looked for a godly person. He found Samuel, told him what was going on, and stayed with him.

This is a good example for us today. When we face challenges and don't know what to do, it's helpful to seek out a wise, godly person. Talk to them about what's going on and ask their advice. If possible, stay close to that person, because being around other Christians gives us strength and courage. When you feel afraid or simply don't know what you should do next, find the godliest person you know, and let their wisdom help guide your next steps.

Dear Father, please put godly people in my life so I'll always have someone to turn to when I need help. Amen.

FOLLOWING THROUGH

Then they told David, "See, the Philistines are fighting against Keilah. They are taking the grain from the grain-floors." So David asked the Lord, "Should I go and fight these Philistines?" And the Lord said to David, "Go, fight the Philistines, and save Keilah."

1 SAMUEL 23:1–2

When faced with a difficult situation, David asked the Lord what to do. The men who reported to David were afraid of the Philistines, and they didn't want to fight them. But David didn't cave in to peer pressure. He listened to what God told him, and he obeyed. God told him to go to Keilah and fight the Philistines. He promised David that if he did this scary thing, he would win. It would have been easy for David to seek God but then disagree and say, "No, God! That doesn't make sense. The Philistines are bigger and stronger than we are." But he didn't do that. He listened to and obeyed God.

When we find ourselves in a difficult situation and we don't know what to do, it's important to seek God and then follow through by obeying Him.

Dear Father, give me strength and courage to listen to You and obey Your voice. Amen.

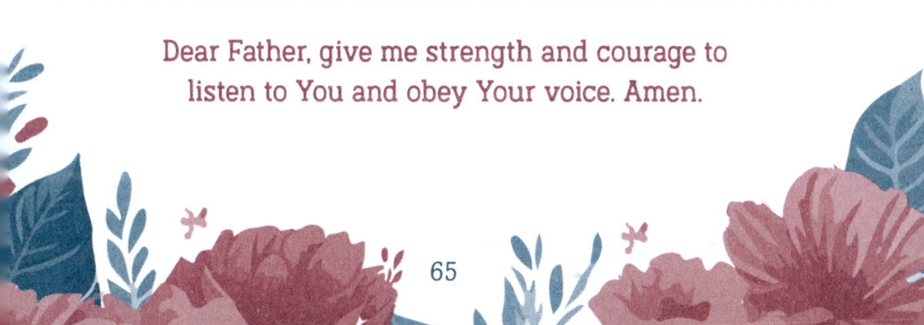

BE KIND ANYWAY

"May the Lord judge between you and me.
May He punish you for your action against me.
But my hand will not be against you."

1 Samuel 24:12

David ran from Saul for a long time. Saul was jealous of David and tried to kill him. One day David was hiding in a cave when Saul came inside. He didn't know David was there, but David was sneaky and cut off a corner of Saul's robe. After Saul left, David called out and showed the corner of the robe. He said, "I could have killed you, but I didn't. Please stop chasing me." But David knew Saul would not stop. Instead of getting even with Saul, David chose to let God handle Saul's punishment.

When people are mean, we shouldn't try to get even. That will only make us angry and bitter. We should keep being kind and let God take care of the punishment.

Dear Father, when others are mean to me,
I want to act the same way. Help me to be kind
even when others aren't. Remind me that it's
Your job to punish others, not mine. Amen.

ASK BEFORE ACTING

Then David asked the Lord, "Should I go after this army? Should I meet them in battle?" The Lord said to him, "Go after them, for you will catch them for sure. And you will be sure to save all the people."

1 SAMUEL 30:8

In this verse, David had just learned that his family and the wives and children of all his soldiers had been captured. He was so upset! To make things worse, his men blamed him for what happened. David probably wanted to run after his family right away, but he didn't. Instead, he asked God for wisdom. Even though he was angry and sad and overwhelmed, he knew better than to act without first asking God what to do.

Too often we act before we pray, and the results are not good. It's important to follow David's example. When we're desperate and overwhelmed, we need to seek God and obey what He says.

Dear Father, when I'm upset, I often react without taking time to talk to You. Teach me to seek Your wisdom before I act in anger or desperation. Amen.

INFLUENCE

Happy is the man who does not walk in the way sinful men tell him to, or stand in the path of sinners, or sit with those who laugh at the truth. But he finds joy in the Law of the Lord and thinks about His Law day and night.

PSALM 1:1–2

Who do you let influence you? Our friends and family influence many of us. Sometimes we try to act like people we see on television or on the internet. Whoever or whatever we spend the most time with usually has the most influence over us. These verses tell us not to let ungodly people have power over us. We shouldn't let them guide the way we think or act. Instead, we should spend our days thinking about God's Word and how much He loves us.

When we find joy in God—so much that we think about Him all the time—He influences our thoughts. And when God controls our thoughts, our lives will be filled with peace, joy, and all good things.

Dear Father, help me stay away from people who don't honor You. I love You with all my heart. Amen.

HEADS UP!

But You, O Lord, are a covering around me, my shining-greatness, and the One Who lifts my head.

Psalm 3:3

Have you ever noticed that when you feel sad or depressed, you walk with your head down? God doesn't want us going through life with our heads down. Instead, He wants us to understand that we're His children! He is the King of kings, and that makes us members of His royal family.

Have you ever seen a prince or princess walking around, shoulders drooped, head to the ground? Probably not. People of royal descent stand up straight and hold their heads high because they know their worth. Princes and princesses understand that their value isn't as much in who they are as it is in who their parents are. Our Father is God, and we should stand tall, hold our shoulders back, and look people in the eye. We can take comfort and courage in knowing He surrounds us, He shines through us, and He wants everyone to know we are His.

Dear Father, thank You for making me a member of Your royal family. When I feel sad or afraid, remind me of who I am through You, and lift my head. Amen.

HE LISTENS

Know that the Lord has set apart him who is God-like for Himself. The Lord hears when I call to Him.

PSALM 4:3

When we imitate God, we become Godlike, or godly. God loves it when we act like Him by being humble and kind and by showing love to the people around us. When we make a habit of acting like Him, He puts His stamp on us and sets us apart from the crowd. He says, "She's mine." And when one of His special, set-apart children calls to Him, He listens to every word. He leans forward with interest to hear what we have to say.

James 5:16 tells us that the prayers of a righteous, godly person are powerful and effective. If you ever wonder if God hears your prayers, you can ask yourself if you're imitating Him in the way you act. And you can know, without doubt, He listens to every word.

Dear Father, I want to be a righteous, godly person. I want to imitate You in my thoughts and actions. Thank You for setting me apart and listening to my prayers. Amen.

WHO AM I?

When I look up and think about Your heavens, the work of Your fingers, the moon and the stars, which You have set in their place, what is man, that You think of him, the son of man that You care for him?

Psalm 8:3–4

Have you ever just stopped and looked at all the amazing things God created? Everything we can see exists because God made it or because God gave someone the ability to make it. Nothing would exist without Him. He can have anything He wants. If He desires something, He can just make it! Imagine this: God, who can have anything He desires, desires you and me most. Wow!

When David wrote this psalm, he asked, "Who am I, that someone as great as You would think of and care about me?" That kind of love is beyond our human understanding. But we don't need to understand it to accept it. (We may not understand how a car runs, but we accept that it does.) We should spend time each day thanking God for loving us.

Dear Father, thank You for loving me. I don't understand Your love, but I'm so grateful for it. Amen.

WITH ALL MY HEART

I will give thanks to the Lord with all my heart. I will tell of all the great things You have done. I will be glad and full of joy because of You. I will sing praise to Your name, O Most High.

Psalm 9:1–2

David was a musician. He played the harp and sang songs to God. In this song, David wrote the words that were in his heart: *I will thank You with everything that's in me. I will tell everyone how great You are. I will be happy, not sad, because of You. I will sing Your praises.*

We don't have to be musically talented to praise God. We can use whatever talents we possess. Whether we're good cooks, gifted athletes, or something else, we can do everything to honor God. We can thank Him and tell others how great God is. And we can remember that no matter what happens, we can be glad and have joy because God loves us.

Dear Father, like David, I want to thank You with all my heart. I want to tell others about how great You are. Because I am Your child, I will be glad even when things don't go my way. Amen.

WHERE ARE YOU?

Why do You stand far away, O Lord?
Why do You hide Yourself in times of trouble?

PSALM 10:1

Have you ever felt like God was ignoring you? Maybe you asked Him for help or for an answer to prayer and He didn't answer right away. Or maybe He didn't answer the way you wanted Him to. God knows we're human and we get frustrated. It's okay to question Him.

It's not okay to be disrespectful to God. But when we don't understand something, it's all right to tell Him so. We can say, "God, where are You? I don't feel like You're listening to me. It doesn't even feel like You're here right now." You can be certain that He always hears your prayers and that He will never leave you. But He also wants you to be honest with Him. Sometimes He may hold out His answer because He wants you to come closer to Him. More than anything, He wants to spend time with you. Talk to Him. Question Him. He is right there, and He hears every word.

Dear Father, thank You for the assurance
that even when it feels like You're hiding,
You love me and will never leave me. Amen.

RIGHT AND GOOD

For the Lord is right and good. He loves what is right and good. And those who are right with Him will see His face.

PSALM 11:7

God is righteous, which means He always does what is right and good. He loves it when His children are righteous. This verse promises that when we do what's right and good, we will see His face. That means we'll have a personal, close relationship with Him.

We might ask ourselves, "Do I always do what is right and good?" The answer is no. We've all sinned, and we've all made poor choices. God knows we're human and we make mistakes. But He loves it when we try. He loves it when, overall, we want to do the right thing. We choose kindness when being mean would be easier. We choose hard work when being lazy is easier. We choose to tell the truth even if it gets us in trouble. When we make a habit of doing what's right and good, God leans near to us, and we have a close relationship with Him.

Dear Father, I want to be close to You. Help me do what is right and good even when it's hard. Amen.

GETTING NOTICED

The Lord has looked down from heaven on the sons of men,
to see if there are any who understand and look for God.

PSALM 14:2

God watches everything. He sits on His throne in heaven and searches for people who love Him and want to know Him more. Many people spend their time thinking about *themselves* and what *they* want. They fill their lives trying to make money or have fun or do whatever makes them feel good.

The Bible tells us that most people don't spend much time thinking about God. So when God finds someone who loves Him, someone who wants to know Him more, He gets excited. He says, "There! That one. I want that person for Myself." Then He brings us into His family and adopts us as His children. If we want God to notice us, all we need to do is look for Him. Talk to Him. Spend time thinking about Him and thanking Him for all the good things He's done.

Dear Father, this verse says You're searching for people who want to know You. I want Your eyes to stop on me. I love You and I want to know You more. Amen.

GOD'S "IN CROWD"

O Lord, who may live in Your tent? Who may live on Your holy hill? He who walks without blame and does what is right and good, and speaks the truth in his heart. He does not hurt others with his tongue, or do wrong to his neighbor, or bring shame to his friend.

PSALM 15:1–3

God loves everyone, but He is especially close to righteous people. These are people who choose to do the right, godly thing.

This passage starts out by asking who is allowed to come into God's presence. Who does God invite to hang out with Him in His personal space? The answer to that question is found in the following sentences. The person who has good character, who tells the truth, who doesn't hurt other people or cause harm—these are people God calls His close friends. If we want to be in God's "in crowd," we can make choices that will bring Him close.

Dear Father, I want to be known for doing the right thing. Help me develop good character. Help me show love to others even when it's hard. I want to live in Your presence and be in Your "in crowd." Amen.

THE WAY TO HAPPINESS

You will show me the way of life. Being with You is to be full of joy. In Your right hand there is happiness forever.

PSALM 16:11

Do you want to be happy? Most people would answer that question with a strong "Yes!" Many people find temporary happiness through money or things or friends or events. But money gets spent, and the thrill doesn't last long. Things get old and wear out. Friends move on to new chapters in their lives, and sometimes they disappoint us. And events, like going to a concert, only last a little while.

If we want lasting happiness, we should stay close to God. When we have a close relationship with God, we can find peace and joy even during difficult times. His way is always the best way and will eventually lead to a satisfying, purpose-filled, joyous life.

Dear Father, thank You for Your Word, which shows me the way to a joy-filled life. Thank You for Your Holy Spirit, who guides me when I don't know what to do. If I ever try to stray away from You, please pull me back into Your presence. Amen.

THE SHADOW OF HIS WINGS

Keep me safe as You would Your own eye.
Hide me in the shadow of Your wings.
PSALM 17:8

David spent many of his young adult years running and hiding from King Saul, who wanted to kill him. While he hid in caves and crevices, he wrote prayers and poems. He asked God to keep him safe. He needed God to hide him so Saul wouldn't find him.

When a bird hides her chicks under her wings, most people never know the chicks are there. They are completely covered and safe. When God protects us, His protection is complete. But if we wander away from Him, we leave His protection. It's important to stay close to God, because His presence shelters us from many of the hard things of this world. Though we may still experience bad things in life, we are always better off in His presence than away from Him.

Dear Father, I want to stay close to You. Hide me in the shadow of Your wings like a bird hides her chicks. Thank You for protecting and taking care of me. Amen.

BLAMELESS BEFORE GOD

Before Him I was without blame. And I have kept myself from sin. So the Lord has paid me back for being right with Him, and for my hands being clean in His eyes.

PSALM 18:23–24

This psalm of David is a song in which he praised God for taking care of him, and he knew the *reason* God had protected him. It was because David stayed close to God. He honored God in all his choices, and he consulted God for all his decisions. During this time in his life, David was without blame. He avoided doing things God wouldn't approve of, and because of this, God watched over him.

When we find ourselves in trouble because of our poor choices, we can still call on God, but we also must acknowledge our part in it. There are often consequences for our behavior. But when we are blameless, we can trust that God sees us and that He will ultimately take care of us.

Dear Father, help me to remain blameless. Like David, I want to honor You with my choices and consult You for my decisions. I love You. Amen.

GIVE THANKS

*So I will give thanks to You among the nations,
O Lord. And I will sing praises to Your name.*

PSALM 18:49

Have you ever thought about all you have to be grateful for? Some things are obvious. We should thank God for giving us life. We should thank Him for giving us food to eat, clothes to wear, and a good place to sleep. But our blessings don't stop there! Every day God blesses us.

If we make a habit of looking for good things, we will find His goodness everywhere! Beautiful flowers, birds and other animals, fluffy clouds, a friend who smiles at us—these are all things we can thank God for. When we praise God and thank Him for all the good things He's done, other people notice and want to know Him too. Start a list of the things you're grateful for, and add to it each day. As you write, praise God for blessing you in so many ways.

Dear Father, thank You for all the good
things in my life. I'm grateful for each one,
and I praise You with all my heart. Amen.

WORDS AND THOUGHTS

Let the words of my mouth and the thoughts of my heart be pleasing in Your eyes, O Lord, my Rock and the One Who saves me.

PSALM 19:14

Did you know that your thoughts can become your words and actions? We can't always control the thoughts that enter our minds, but we can control how long we dwell on each one.

In 2 Corinthians 10:5, Paul instructed his readers to take control of every thought. When a thought shows up in our minds that we know isn't pleasing to God, we're supposed to tell that thought to go away. We can turn our minds to better things, to things that make God happy. When we do this, we train ourselves to focus on good things instead of bad ones. When we fill our minds with good things by reading God's Word, listening to music that honors Him, and thinking about Him, we naturally talk about Him and act in ways that please Him. Do your best, today and every day, to turn your thoughts to God and speak in a way that honors Him.

Dear Father, I want my thoughts and words to honor You today. Amen.

TRUST IN GOD

Some trust in wagons and some in horses. But we will trust in the name of the Lord, our God. They have fallen on their knees. But we rise up and stand straight.

PSALM 20:7–8

During Bible times, armies used wagons and horses. The more wagons and horses an army had, the more powerful it was. But all the wagons and horses in the world can't stand against God!

Today people might trust in different things to give them security. Some might trust in money, success, or fame. Some might trust in friends and family. Those are good to have, but none of them compare to God's power. Each of those can disappear or fail us, but God will never fail. When we trust in God alone for our strength, we will always end up on the winning team. Those other things will eventually lose their power, but God will sustain us so that at the end of it all we will stand.

Dear Father, I trust You for everything in my life. Thank You for being my strength and helping me stand through every hard thing that comes my way. Amen.

GOD'S ADDRESS

Yet You are holy. The praises Israel gives You are Your throne.

PSALM 22:3

Have you ever felt far away from God? Perhaps you had a bad day or week and you wondered why God disappeared. There is a foolproof way to find God when we don't know where He is. This verse tells us His personal address. He lives in the praises of His people! He loves it when we praise Him. He loves praise so much, He has placed His throne right in the middle of it. That's where He sits, where He rules, where He does all His business.

If you ever find yourself wondering where God is, praise Him. Tell Him how wonderful He is. Fill your heart and mind with thoughts of how amazing, generous, and kind He has been to you and others. Praise Him, and you'll find yourself in His presence. When He hears you praising Him, He leans closer and listens to every word.

Dear Father, thank You for giving me Your personal address. When I feel far away from Your presence, remind me to praise You. Amen.

HOPE

Yes, let no one who hopes in You be put to shame.
But put to shame those who hurt others without a reason.

PSALM 25:3

The word *hope* means a belief that something good is waiting in the future. When we hope for something, that means we haven't received that thing yet. We're still waiting on the good thing to happen, but we know in our hearts that it's coming. In this verse, David says, "God, I believe in Your goodness. I know You won't let me down or make me feel embarrassed because You didn't come through."

Those who put their faith in God will never be disappointed. He may not act exactly the way we want Him to, but the end result will be even better than we could imagine! But those who are mean to others, who hurt innocent people on purpose, and who don't live to please God—those people will be ashamed in the end. God will punish the wicked, but He won't let His children down.

Dear Father, I believe in Your goodness, and I know You won't let me down. Thank You for taking care of me and giving me a reason to hope. Amen.

SHARING SECRETS

The secret of the Lord is for those who fear Him.
And He will make them know His agreement.

PSALM 25:14

Do you have a best friend with whom you share secrets? Secret sharing is something we do with the people we trust the most. When we treat God with reverence and respect, He calls us His friends. He invites us into His inner circle and shares His secrets with us.

Many people struggle to understand God and His ways. But when we really want to know Him, when we truly respect God and want to please Him, He helps us understand things that other people don't understand. God doesn't care how smart we are, how much money we have, or how talented or successful we may be. When God looks for His closest friends, He looks for people who love Him, honor Him, and live in a way that pleases Him.

Dear Father, more than anything, I want to be Your friend. I want to know and understand You. Please share Your secrets with me so I can know You better. Amen.

HERE AND NOW

I would have been without hope if I had not believed that I would see the loving-kindness of the Lord in the land of the living. Wait for the Lord. Be strong. Let your heart be strong. Yes, wait for the Lord.

PSALM 27:13–14

It's nice to think about heaven, isn't it? When we get to heaven, there will be no more tears, no more pain, no more bad things ever. We'll spend eternity in God's physical presence, and it will be better than we can imagine!

But we don't have to wait for heaven to experience God's goodness. His love and kindness are for the land of the living. That means they're for us, right here, right now. Sometimes we have to wait for God to see what He will do. The waiting can be hard. But we can wait with hope, not fear. We can wait with expectation, knowing that God has something wonderful in store for those who love Him.

Dear Father, thank You for this reminder that Your goodness is for me right now. I don't have to wait until heaven to receive Your blessings. Give me patience as I wait for You to act. Amen.

WHEN WE MESS UP

When I kept quiet about my sin, my bones wasted away from crying all day long. For day and night Your hand was heavy upon me. My strength was dried up as in the hot summer.

PSALM 32:3–4

Have you ever done something wrong, something you knew you shouldn't have done? Did you try to keep it a secret? We've all done that at some point. But when we hold on to our sin and try to keep it from God, it makes us miserable. We feel guilty and ashamed. We don't feel right because we aren't right with God.

There's no point in hiding things from God. He knows everything anyway. When we take responsibility for our sin by admitting it to God and asking for forgiveness, and by trying to make things right with people we've hurt, we'll feel like a big weight has been lifted. We all make mistakes. When that happens, it's important to go to God right away, confess what we did wrong, and draw close to Him once again.

Dear Father, help me stay away from sin.
When I do mess up, remind me to make things right
with You and others as soon as possible. Amen.

HOPE IN GOD

O Lord, let Your loving-kindness be upon us as we put our hope in You.

PSALM 33:22

Did you know that many people feel anxious and afraid all the time? Even if they appear confident and self-assured, they may have things deep inside that cause them to worry. Most bullies are mean because they're trying to cover up for something they're afraid of.

Hope is the opposite of fear and anxiety. When we know God, we have hope, or a belief that good things are in store. Those who have a close relationship with God can act based on hope instead of fear. When you feel afraid, remind yourself that God is in control. He loves you and has wonderful plans for your life. When you meet someone who doesn't seem to have hope, try to share your hope with them. Be kind and show love, and if you have a chance, tell them how great God is.

Dear Father, thank You that I can put my hope in You. Help me shine Your hope and love to others. Amen.

GUIDELINES

Come, you children, listen to me. I will teach you the fear of the Lord. Who is the man who has a desire for life, and wants to live long so that he may see good things? Keep your tongue from sin and your lips from speaking lies. Turn away from what is sinful. Do what is good. Look for peace and follow it.

PSALM 34:11–14

David wrote many things just for God. In these verses, he wrote for his children and for the people in his kingdom. He wanted them to understand how to live the best life possible. He listed the character traits that lead to a long, happy life. First, treat God with honor and respect. Next, always be honest and truthful. Third, stay away from sin, or anything that offends God. Finally, always try to live at peace with those around you. Because we live in a world where bad things exist, people who follow these principles will still have problems. But overall, these guidelines will help us live happier, more peaceful lives.

Dear Father, help me follow these guidelines in the choices I make. I want to honor You, speak the truth, avoid sin, and live peacefully with others. Amen.

YOUNG AND OLD

I have been young, and now I am old. Yet I have never seen the man who is right with God left alone, or his children begging for bread. All day long he is kind and lets others use what he has. And his children make him happy.

Psalm 37:25–26

It's easy to look at older people and think they don't know what they're talking about. We think they don't understand what we're going through. But the truth is, older people understand a lot because they've been through a lot.

David wrote this passage when he was older, and he said he'd never seen God turn His back on those who lived to please Him. Instead, David noticed that those who are right with God seem happier. They are kind and generous, and for the most part, they have good relationships with the people they care about. By living in a way that honors God, we bring about good things for ourselves and our families. When we honor God, we can be certain He'll never let us down.

Dear Father, thank You for being reliable and for always taking care of me. Help me live in a way that pleases You. Amen.

GOSSIP

*All who hate me speak in secret together against me.
They make plans to hurt me, saying, "A bad thing has come over him. When he lies down, he will not rise again."*

PSALM 41:7–8

While David was on the run from Saul, he didn't always know whom he could trust. He saw people talking, and he felt sure some of them were saying bad things about him. When we talk about other people in a way that's not nice, it's called gossip. Gossip hurts.

The Bible tells us in James 3 that the tongue is a powerful weapon. When we fail to control our words, we can inflict deep wounds on others that could take years to heal. When someone comes to us with interesting information about another person, it's only natural to want to listen. But we must train ourselves to walk away or change the subject. Even if the information is true, if it's not kind or necessary, we shouldn't take part in it. As God's children, we are to show only love. Love does not intentionally say or do things that hurt others.

Dear Father, I'm sorry for hurtful things I've said about others. Help me avoid gossip. Amen.

THIRSTY

As the deer desires rivers of water,
so my soul desires You, O God.

Psalm 42:1

David wrote many of the psalms, but not all of them. The sons of Korah wrote this chapter. Years before, this family rebelled against Moses. Most were killed, but some of them survived. Their descendants repented. They wanted another chance to serve God.

God loves mercy, and when we're sorry for our sins, He always gives us a second chance. This family became the choir or praise team. They wrote these beautiful words that have been sung by many worshippers ever since biblical times: "As the deer desires rivers of water, so my soul desires You, O God." When deer run around, they get hot and thirsty. They need water. Have you ever been hot and thirsty? Did you long for something cold to drink? That's how we should long for God. We need Him to quench our thirst for love, for mercy, and for righteousness. Next time you reach for a glass of water, think about God and how much you need Him in your life.

Dear Father, I need You like I need water.
Thank You for loving me. Amen.

BRAGGING ON GOD

In God we have had our pride all day long.
And we will give thanks to Your name forever.
PSALM 44:8

What does it mean to have pride in something? It means we want others to know how great something is. When our parents are proud of us, they may tell others and boast about us. It feels nice when someone is proud of us! God loves it when we brag and boast about Him. He wants us to tell others how great He is.

How often do you boast about God? How often do you tell your friends and family about the great things He does for you every single day? Ask God to show you reasons to brag on Him. And ask Him to create natural opportunities to talk about Him with others so it doesn't feel awkward or forced. The more you brag on God, the easier it will become.

Dear Father, You've given me many reasons to tell others about how great You are. Help me recognize opportunities to tell of Your greatness, and let those around me listen and want to know You more. Amen.

GOD, OUR HELPER

God is our safe place and our strength. He is always our help when we are in trouble. So we will not be afraid, even if the earth is shaken and the mountains fall into the center of the sea, and even if its waters go wild with storm and the mountains shake with its action.

PSALM 46:1–3

Have you ever needed help? Have you found yourself in a hard situation and you didn't know what to do? Perhaps you felt afraid or frustrated.

Even when no one else is around, God is there. We can always call to Him when we're in trouble, when we don't feel safe, or when we feel too weak to do anything. He loves His children, and He will always help us when we need it. He may not always prevent a bad thing from happening, but He will walk with us through the trouble. He will hold our hand and give us comfort and strength. Even when He doesn't take away the problem, He helps us get through it.

Dear Father, thank You for always being there. When I'm troubled, when I'm tired or afraid, remind me that You're right there with me. Amen.

BE STILL

Be quiet and know that I am God. I will be honored among the nations. I will be honored in the earth.

PSALM 46:10

Has anyone ever told you to be still? Sometimes it's hard. There are so many things we want to do, people we want to see, places we want to go. But do you know what's even harder than keeping our bodies still? Keeping our minds and thoughts still can be super hard. It's difficult to control what thoughts enter our brains. Sometimes it can feel like a thousand different thoughts compete for our attention.

In this verse, God asks us to quiet our thoughts and focus only on Him. While we can't do this all the time, it's important to keep God present in our thoughts. And sometimes, at least once a day, we should push everything else aside and think about how amazing, how loving, and how good God is.

Dear Father, teach me to be still in my mind. Help me learn to quiet my thoughts and focus only on You. You are amazing. You are so, so good. I love You with all my heart. Amen.

LOVING-KINDNESS

Show me loving-kindness, O God, show me loving-kindness. For my soul goes to You to be safe. And I will be safe in the shadow of Your wings until the trouble has passed.

PSALM 57:1

Have you ever held a newborn baby? Perhaps you've held a sibling or someone else you knew. Maybe you held a young puppy or kitten. Babies are helpless and delicate, and when we hold them, we must be extra gentle. Some people are so moved with love and kindness when they hold a baby that they sing soft songs. They cuddle the baby, and they act in a way that shows gentle care. That's how God treats us! We are His children, and He shows us tender affection.

In this psalm, David asked God to show loving-kindness. He said, "Remember that I'm Your child. Be tender and merciful to me." When we feel afraid, or when we face trouble of any kind, we can call out to God to keep us safe. He will show us His tender care because He loves us so.

Dear Father, thank You for showing me loving-kindness. I know I'm always safe in Your arms. Amen.

NOT ALONE

My God in His loving-kindness will meet me. God will let me look at those who come against me and know that I will win the fight.

Psalm 59:10

Have you ever felt like others were against you? Maybe you've faced a bully at school or a mean person who laughs when they hurt others. When you're faced with a situation where someone wants to hurt you and you don't know how to respond, call out to God. He will send His Holy Spirit to help you know how to behave in each situation. He'll give you the words to say to a bully. He'll help you know when to stand and fight and when to get far away from the situation. Most importantly, He will stand with you, and you won't be alone.

Facing an enemy is never easy, but you can always know that God is right beside you. With God on your side, you can know that in the end you'll be the winner.

Dear Father, when I face difficult people and situations, remind me of Your presence. Give me wisdom to know how to respond. Amen.

NOT GREATLY SHAKEN

He alone is my rock and the One Who saves me.
He is my strong place. I will not be shaken.

PSALM 62:2

When we stay close to God, it's like we're standing on a solid rock. Rock isn't like sand. It won't shift easily. When we stand on a boulder, we know we're safe from life's storms. Another translation of the Bible calls God "my fortress," and it says, "I shall not be greatly shaken" (ESV).

Sometimes life shakes us. Sometimes we're affected by difficult circumstances. Those situations challenge us. They change us and help us grow. The hard things in life may cause some bumps and bruises. We may get hurt. We might even cry a little, but that's okay. We may be shaken, but we won't be *greatly* shaken. With God on our side, we are safe and sound. At the end of it all, we will stand stronger than ever.

Dear Father, thank You for being my rock and my fortress. When I feel shaken by life, remind me that I'm not greatly shaken. In the end, I'll be just fine as long as You're by my side. Amen.

NEAR GOD

But as for me, it is good to be near God.
I have made the Lord God my safe place.
So I may tell of all the things You have done.

Psalm 73:28

A man named Asaph wrote this psalm. He was one of the music leaders in the temple, and he wrote songs and poems. In this verse, he talked about how much he loved to be near God. Do you have a close friend you like to spend time with? When we're with our true friends, we feel safe. We enjoy spending time with them. Asaph enjoyed spending time with God, and we should too.

We will never have a truer, closer friend than God. He knows everything about us, and He thinks we're amazing! We never have to worry about Him hurting us. His actions are always based on His great love for us. God longs to be near you, and He wants to be near your friends too. Whenever you have a chance, tell others about God. Introduce them to Him so they can know Him too.

Dear Father, I love being close to You.
Thank You for being my safe place. Amen.

DO IT NOW

Teach us to understand how many days we have.
Then we will have a heart of wisdom to give You.

Psalm 90:12

When we're young, it's easy to think we have plenty of time to do whatever we want. It's easy to put off the important things until later. Many people think they'll get right with God or develop a close relationship with Him—*later*. But ask any older person, and they'll tell you life is short. It goes by really fast.

If something is important to you, you should do it now. Show the people you love how much they mean to you—now. Work toward the important goals you have—now. Study your Bible and grow in your relationship with God—right now and every day for as long as you live. Ask God to help you understand your purpose in life—to love Him and love others—and make it a point to live out that purpose every single day.

Dear Father, help me understand that life is a precious gift. Help me make the most of every day as I live out Your purpose for me. Amen.

BECAUSE SHE LOVES ME

Because he has loved Me, I will bring him out of trouble. I will set him in a safe place on high, because he has known My name. He will call upon Me, and I will answer him. I will be with him in trouble. I will take him out of trouble and honor him. I will please him with a long life. And I will show him My saving power.

PSALM 91:14–16

A lot of people claim to know God when it's the popular thing to do. Yet they often live like strangers to God when it's convenient. God notices the way we live. He sees the choices we make every day. When we live each day out of love for Him, He is faithful to take care of us. When we have a close relationship with Him, He is loyal to that consistent faith. When He sees we're in trouble, He says, "Because (your name) loves Me, I will help her through this situation. I'll make sure she's taken care of because she's one of My special ones."

Dear Father, I love You. I want to honor You in all that I do. Amen.

A NEW SONG

Sing to the Lord a new song. Let all the earth sing to the Lord.

PSALM 96:1

It's fun to sing worship songs we learn in church or hear on the radio. But have you ever sung a *new* song to God? He loves it when we make up songs about Him. They can be serious or silly. It doesn't matter, as long as we sing about our sincere love for Him. What great thing has He done for you? Write a song about it! Or do something else creative—draw a picture, write a poem, create a puppet show.

God is a creative God, and He made us in His image. He loves it when we do creative things for Him. It doesn't have to be perfect. You don't have to show it to anybody but God unless you want to. Think of something fun and creative you can do for God today to show Him how much you love Him.

Dear Father, I want to show You how much I love You in all I do. Help me sing a new song for You today. Amen.

LIFESTYLE CHOICE

The name of the Lord is to be praised from the time the sun rises to when it sets.

PSALM 113:3

On page 83 of this book, we learned God's address. He lives in our praise! This verse tells us to praise Him all day long. Every moment we're awake, we should praise God. That doesn't mean we have to praise Him out loud—though we should if it's appropriate. But we should also praise Him in our thoughts. We should walk around with an attitude of praise. This kind of praise is a constant choice we make. It's a lifestyle.

Praising God takes the focus off ourselves and places it where it belongs: on God. Do you have a lifestyle of praise? Ask God to occupy your thoughts today as you make the choice to live with an attitude of praise.

Dear Father, when I open my eyes in the morning, remind me to praise You. When I go to sleep at night, I want to praise You. And every moment in between, I want my thoughts to focus on how wonderful You are. Amen.

NEGATIVE PEOPLE

I have lived too long with those who hate peace.
I am for peace. But when I speak, they are for war.

PSALM 120:6–7

Have you ever been around someone who wants to argue all the time? Maybe they pick fights with you. Or perhaps they try to be your friend but they start arguments with other people. Some people have negative attitudes, and they'll try to make those around them have bad attitudes too. It's best to avoid these people.

Perhaps someone is usually positive but they have a bad day. Don't let their attitude bring you down. Stay peaceful and positive! And if you notice someone is always in an argument with someone else, stay away from that person. Be kind. Show love. But don't allow negative people to become your close friends. Instead, show them what it looks like to be kind, gentle, and at peace with everyone.

Dear Father, help me not to get sucked into arguments and negative attitudes. Help me avoid gossip and unkind words. Make my life an example of Your love and peace for everyone to see. Give me wisdom to stay away from negative people. Amen.

FROM TEARS TO JOY

He who goes out crying as he carries his bag of seed will return with songs of joy as he brings much grain with him.

PSALM 126:6

Have you ever met a farmer? In the spring he sows seed in the ground. If the weather isn't good, he may worry that the seeds will never sprout. If that happens, he won't have anything to eat in the fall.

This verse tells us that no matter how bad things may look in the beginning, God will turn things around for good for those who love Him. We will go through hard times in our lives. Being a Christian doesn't shield us from ever shedding tears. But the end result will always be joy and gladness for those who love God with their whole hearts. Next time you face something hard, next time you shed tears, remind yourself that your story isn't finished yet. God will make sure your story has a happy ending.

Dear Father, thank You for writing my story. I trust You for the ending, and I know it will be a good one. Amen.

LIVING IN UNITY

See, how good and how pleasing it is for brothers to live together as one! It is like oil of great worth poured on the head, flowing down through the hair on the face, even the face of Aaron, and flowing down to his coat.

PSALM 133:1–2

Do you have siblings? How about cousins or a group of friends? Anytime a group of people live together or spend a lot of time together, they are bound to have disagreements and misunderstandings. But it's important to do all in our power to live in unity with the people around us.

When two people can't get along, it affects everyone else in the house or in the group. But when everyone looks out for everyone else, when each person in the group treats the other with kindness, compassion, and love, everyone in the group feels happy and safe and loved. A peaceful home is like a rare treasure. Make sure you're doing your part to create that kind of treasure for yourself and those you love.

Dear Father, help me do my part to live at peace with my family and friends. Amen.

SEND ME

Then I heard the voice of the Lord, saying, "Whom should I send? Who will go for Us?" Then I said, "Here am I. Send me!"

ISAIAH 6:8

God has compassion on people. When He sees people suffer, He wants to help them. God is love, and He can't help but love people. He relies on us to show that love in a real, up-close, and personal way. The world is filled with people who are hurting, who need to know Jesus loves them. They need to know they can have a relationship with the almighty God. But how will they know unless we tell them?

God calls each of us to be His messengers. Right now He asks, "Whom should I send? Who will go and tell others of My love?" Our answer should always be, "Here I am, Lord. Send me!"

Dear Father, show me the people I know who are hurting and need to know You. I know people everywhere need to be told about Your love. Here I am, Lord. Send me. Amen.

JOHN'S PURPOSE

John wore clothes made of hair from camels. He had a leather belt around him. His food was locusts and wild honey.

MATTHEW 3:4

John was Jesus' cousin. He was called by God to prepare the way for Jesus. Before Jesus started His public ministry, John went around telling people to get ready. He wanted them to repent of their sins and get right with God so they'd be prepared when they met Jesus. John had an important job to do. He didn't worry about having wealth or nice clothes or fine dining. He wore rags and ate bugs. But God cared tenderly for John's needs. He ate honey from the honeycomb, which was considered a rare treat. Many people probably thought John was strange. But he had a big impact on God's kingdom. Today he is in heaven, and he is probably wearing fancy clothes and eating a feast at God's table. When we live out our purpose for God, we can be certain God will reward us.

Dear Father, forgive me for worrying about things that aren't important. Show me Your purpose for my life, and help me fulfill it.

GOD'S WORD AS A WEAPON

The devil came tempting Him and said, "If You are the Son of God, tell these stones to be made into bread." But Jesus said, "It is written, 'Man is not to live on bread only. Man is to live by every word that God speaks.'"

Matthew 4:3–4

Jesus had been in the desert for forty days with no food. He was praying and getting ready for what God called Him to do—die for our sins. He was really, really hungry. Satan always tempts us when we're weak. He tried to get Jesus to forget about His purpose and make something to eat. Notice how Jesus answered Satan. He quoted God's Word.

We overcome temptation with the Word of God. The more of God's Word we know, the easier it is to say no when Satan tempts us. In Hebrews 4:12 we're told the Word of God is a living, active thing. There is power in God's Word. When we speak His Word, we become stronger and Satan runs!

Dear Father, help me learn Your Word so I can stand strong against Satan. Amen.

MEETING NEEDS

Jesus went over all Galilee. He taught in their places of worship and preached the Good News of the holy nation. He healed all kinds of sickness and disease among the people. The news about Him went over all the country of Syria. They brought all the sick people to Him with many kinds of diseases and pains. They brought to Him those who had demons. They brought those who at times lose the use of their minds. They brought those who could not use their hands and legs. He healed them.

MATTHEW 4:23–24

When Jesus walked the earth, He had compassion on people. He met their practical needs. He didn't just tell them to get right with God. Instead, He saw their needs and He took care of them. He healed them. We should follow His example.

It's important to tell others that God loves them. But they won't understand that love if their practical needs aren't met. Do you know someone who needs a friend? Be that friend. If someone needs something and you have extra, share. People will understand God's love better if we meet their practical needs first.

Dear Father, show me how to meet the practical needs of those around me. Amen.

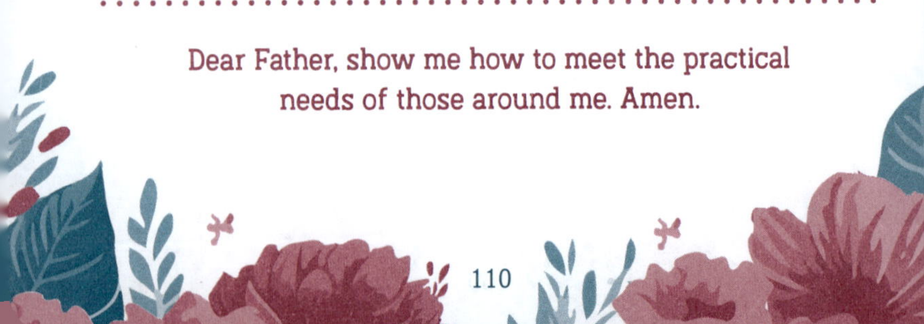

SHINE YOUR LIGHT

"Let your light shine in front of men. Then they will see the good things you do and will honor your Father Who is in heaven."

MATTHEW 5:16

Have you ever noticed how even a small light overcomes darkness? In a dark forest, even a tiny match can be seen from far away. When we show love and compassion to others, when we are kind, and when we do good deeds, we shine our lights. Others are drawn to that light in us, and some could be introduced to God's love because of our actions.

We don't do good things to earn salvation. We do good things *because* of our salvation. We show our thanks to Jesus for His love by acting in a way that honors Him and brings others to Him. Can you think of ways you can shine your light today?

Dear Father, I'm so glad I know You and have Your light inside me. Help me shine Your love to others by being kind, showing love, and always doing the right thing. I want others to see Your light in me and come to You. Amen.

A PURE HEART

"I tell you, unless you are more right with God than the teachers of the Law and the proud religious law-keepers, you will never get into the holy nation of heaven."

MATTHEW 5:20

Righteousness is a trait God loves. It means that we are right with God and that we always try to do the right thing. But self-righteousness is a trait God hates. When people are self-righteous, they think they're better than other people. A self-righteous person tries to look good on the outside, but her heart is not right with God. In biblical times, the scribes and Pharisees were teachers of God's law. They thought that because they were important religious leaders, they were better than other people.

Jesus doesn't care much about how we look on the outside. He's more concerned with what our hearts look like. Spend some time talking to God today, and ask Him to show you what your heart looks like. Ask Him to give you a pure heart.

Dear Father, forgive me for times when I've been self-righteous. Give me a pure heart. Amen.

BECOMING PERFECT

"You must be perfect as your Father in heaven is perfect."
MATTHEW 5:48

Are you perfect? If your answer is no, you're not alone. Nobody is perfect except Jesus Christ. Why would God demand perfection from us, knowing that it's impossible? If you find this passage in your Bible and read the verses right before it, it might make more sense. Some translations say that we *shall be* perfect as our Father in heaven is perfect. He is in the process of making us perfect.

We won't be made completely perfect until we reach heaven, but we can come close to that perfection now by loving others as God loves them. That means loving people even when they're hard to love. It means loving our enemies and praying for people who have hurt us. It's difficult to love like God loves, but He lives in us and He will help us. When we love others even when they're mean to us, we become very much like God.

Dear Father, I want to love perfectly like You love. Help me love others even when it's hard. Amen.

WHEN YOU PRAY

"When you pray, do not say the same thing over and over again making long prayers like the people who do not know God. They think they are heard because their prayers are long. Do not be like them. Your Father knows what you need before you ask Him."

MATTHEW 6:7–8

Some people think that to get what they want, they need to impress God. They think prayers need to be long, with holy-sounding words and language. God probably shakes His head when that happens. He loves it when we talk to Him, whether the conversation is long or short. But we certainly don't need to impress Him. He already knows everything about us. He knows everything we've done and everything we need.

When we talk to God, we should talk to Him like we'd talk to a friend. Casual conversation, where we tell God what's on our minds and listen to Him, is exactly what He wants.

Dear Father, I'm so glad I can come to You just as I am. I'm glad I don't have to try to impress You. Teach me how to pray. Amen.

WHERE IS YOUR TREASURE?

"Do not gather together for yourself riches of this earth. They will be eaten by bugs and become rusted. Men can break in and steal them. Gather together riches in heaven where they will not be eaten by bugs or become rusted. Men cannot break in and steal them. For wherever your riches are, your heart will be there also."

MATTHEW 6:19–21

Do you ever daydream about having more money, nicer clothes, or fancier things? Having money is not wrong. God gives us everything we need. Sometimes He blesses us with more than we need. When that happens, it's for a specific purpose: to bless others. It's easy to get caught up in wanting more for ourselves to use for our own pleasure. When we do that, we're storing up earthly treasures that won't last. But if we use what we have to bless other people, to meet their needs and lift their spirits and introduce them to God, then we store up treasures in heaven. Where are you storing your treasures?

Dear Father, I want to store up treasures in heaven. Show me how You'd like me to bless others today. Amen.

DON'T WORRY

"Do not worry about tomorrow. Tomorrow will have its own worries. The troubles we have in a day are enough for one day."

MATTHEW 6:34

Do you ever think about what might happen tomorrow or next week or next month and get a bad feeling in your stomach? Maybe these thoughts keep you awake at night. That's called worry, and the Bible says it's not something Christians should do. Worrying about things shows that we don't trust God like we should. When we truly believe that He loves us, when we know in our hearts that He is all-powerful and that He will take care of our needs, we can relax. We'll have peace in our hearts and praise on our lips.

Next time you find yourself worrying, try praising God instead. Ask Him to help you trust Him more.

Dear Father, I worry about all sorts of things. I want to learn to trust You more. Forgive me for letting fear control my thoughts. I know You love me, You will take care of me, and You have good things in store for my life. Amen.

ASK FOR ANYTHING

"Ask, and what you are asking for will be given to you. Look, and what you are looking for you will find. Knock, and the door you are knocking on will be opened to you. Everyone who asks receives what he asks for. Everyone who looks finds what he is looking for. Everyone who knocks has the door opened to him."

MATTHEW 7:7–8

Our Father longs to give good things to the people who love Him with all their hearts. When we ask Him for things, believing He loves us, He gets excited. Often He blesses us even beyond what we asked for! Other times He doesn't give us what we ask for because He has something even better in store. He is good and loving and kind, and He knows more than we do. If we ask for something but He knows it won't turn out well for us, He may say no to our request. But He will always give us everything we need to fulfill His purpose for our lives.

Is there something you want or need? Ask God, and trust Him to provide His best for you.

Dear Father, I know I can ask You for anything. I trust Your response. Amen.

DO TO OTHERS

"Do for other people whatever you would like to have them do for you. This is what the Jewish Law and the early preachers said."

MATTHEW 7:12

When we treat others the way we'd like to be treated, we're actually showing love. This one verse above sums up the law and the prophets. That means that if you take everything in God's law and everything God's teachers have said and sum it up in one sentence, this is it.

Treat others the way you'd want to be treated. Be kind. Show compassion. Don't hurt people. Don't kill or steal or gossip. Share your abundance with others who don't have enough. Show interest in others and treat them like they're important. These are just a few ways we show love to others. When we do these things, God is pleased.

Dear Father, teach me to treat others the way I want to be treated even when they don't do the same. I want to please You. Make my life a lamp of Your love for everyone to see. Amen.

GOOD FRUIT

"It is true, every good tree has good fruit. Every bad tree has bad fruit. A good tree cannot have bad fruit. A bad tree cannot have good fruit."

MATTHEW 7:17–18

How would you react if you picked up a big, shiny red apple, took a huge bite, and discovered the inside was rotten and worm infested? Yuck! Most of us would spit it out. Some people look pretty on the outside, but inside their souls are unhealthy. They're not living in a way that pleases God. Read the verse again and ask yourself, "What kind of fruit does my life bear?"

If your actions are characterized by love, kindness, and generosity, good for you! You are bearing good fruit. But if your actions often show an interest in yourself instead of others, if you get angry a lot or do mean things, you might need to ask God to heal you and make your spirit healthy, godly, and pure. More than anything, God wants you to produce good fruit.

Dear Father, I want to bear good fruit. Help me adjust my thoughts and actions to reflect Your love in my life. Amen.

HOW CAN I KNOW?

"Not everyone who says to me, 'Lord, Lord,' will go into the holy nation of heaven. The one who does the things My Father in heaven wants him to do will go into the holy nation of heaven."

MATTHEW 7:21

This is a hard verse to read. It's unpleasant to consider that some people think they'll go to heaven when in reality they won't. But we can know for sure we'll go to heaven if we do what God wants us to do. He doesn't expect us to be perfect. He knows we're human and we make mistakes. When we mess up, He wants us to admit our failures and get back on the road to righteousness. He wants us to recognize that Jesus is God's Son and that He died for our sins then rose from the dead on the third day. Once we've done that, He wants us to love others and do good things. We don't do these things to earn our way to heaven but as a thank-you to God for all He's done for us.

Dear Father, thank You for Jesus and for all You've done for me. I want to honor You in all I do. Amen.

LISTEN AND OBEY

"Whoever hears these words of Mine and does not do them, will be like a foolish man who built his house on sand. The rain came down. The water came up. The wind blew and hit the house. The house fell and broke apart."

MATTHEW 7:26–27

It's easy to get distracted while sitting in church. Our minds think about a hundred different things. But when someone is teaching God's Word, whether it's a pastor, a Sunday school teacher, or a parent, it's important to listen. Nothing is more important than knowing and obeying God's Word. We can't obey His Word if we don't know what it says!

God doesn't want us to hear His Word and then live however we want. When we do that, God says we are foolish and we will have all kinds of trouble in life. He wants us to listen to and obey His Word. When we do, we become wise and God is pleased.

Dear Father, help me to learn Your Word and apply it to my life. I don't want to be foolish and ignore Your Word. Instead, I want to be wise. Help me live the way You want me to. Amen.

RELAX

He said to them, "Why are you afraid? You have so little faith!" Then He stood up. He spoke sharp words to the wind and the waves. Then the wind stopped blowing.

MATTHEW 8:26

Have you ever found yourself in a bad storm? The disciples did. They were in the middle of the sea in a small boat. Thunder pounded and lightning flashed. The wind howled, and the boat tossed this way and that on the waves. When the disciples called for Jesus, He was sound asleep. They woke Him up because they were afraid. Jesus may have yawned, stretched, and said, "What's the big deal?" He'd been asleep because He knew God would take care of them. He told the wind and waves to be still, and the storm stopped.

When we face storms and difficult things in life, we can relax. We can rest easy, knowing our Father controls everything, loves us, and will always take care of us.

Dear Father, forgive me for being afraid when storms and troubles show up in my life. Next time I'm afraid, remind me of who You are. Teach me to relax in Your love and to trust You. Amen.

THE LOAD

"For My way of carrying a load is easy and My load is not heavy."

MATTHEW 11:30

Have you ever carried something heavy? The longer you carry it, the heavier it seems. Another translation of the Bible says, "My yoke is easy" (NRSV). A yoke is a wooden piece that is placed over the necks of two animals—often farm animals. The yoke joins the animals so they can work together to pull a piece of equipment. A good farmer will make each side of the yoke specifically to fit that animal's neck. If the yoke doesn't fit, it will rub and cause pain.

When Jesus said, "My yoke is easy," He didn't mean we won't have a load to carry. He meant that our load is specially designed for each of us. Our load won't hurt us. Instead, it will help us live out His purpose for us. And He promises to walk beside us and help us carry the load.

Dear Father, thank You for designing my load especially for me, to help me grow into the person You created me to be. Thank You for walking beside me and helping me with my load. Amen.

THE ACCUSER

The proud religious law-keepers saw this.
They said to Jesus, "See! Your followers do
what the Law says not to do on the Day of Rest."

MATTHEW 12:2

Jesus and His disciples had worked hard speaking to the crowds, healing people, and sharing God's love. They were tired and hungry. They walked through a field and picked a little of the grain to eat. But it was the Sabbath, and Jewish people weren't supposed to gather anything from the fields on that day. The religious people didn't like Jesus, so they looked for anything to accuse Him of.

The Bible tells us that Satan is the accuser. When we look for others to mess up, when we try to find fault with others so we can gossip about them or make them feel ashamed, we align ourselves with Satan. It is God's place to judge others and find fault. It is our place to share God's love.

Dear Father, forgive me for the times I've tried to find fault with someone else. Teach me to treat others the way I want to be treated. Teach me to love like You love. Amen.

ONLY LOVE

"A good man will speak good things because of the good in him. A bad man will speak bad things because of the sin in him. I say to you, on the day men stand before God, they will have to give an answer for every word they have spoken that was not important."

MATTHEW 12:35–36

There's an old saying that goes, "Sticks and stones may break my bones, but words will never hurt me." That's a fun rhyme, but it's not true. Words can hurt much worse than sticks and stones. While physical bruises heal with time, unkind words can remain in a person's memory forever. They can cause great pain each time the memory surfaces.

Words are powerful, and we must be careful to speak only good, encouraging things. God has given us an important message to share—the message that God loves people more than they can think or imagine. We should never say things that make others feel hurt or unloved. To the best of our ability, we should speak only words that deliver the message of God's love to others.

Dear Father, help me guard my words and speak only Your love to others.

THE TREASURE

"The holy nation of heaven is like a box of riches buried in a field. A man found it and then hid it again. In his joy he goes and sells all that he has and buys that field."

MATTHEW 13:44

In this story, a man sells everything he has to buy a certain field because he knows the value of what's buried in that field. He knows it's worth giving up everything for. He'll receive it all back and much, much more! Heaven is like that field. It contains great treasure. It's worth giving up everything for because we'll end up with everything we gave up plus a whole lot more. It is worth giving up whatever is required to please God and be a part of His kingdom.

Every treasure, every goal, every ambition you have—give it all up for the Creator. Nothing in this world can compare to being called God's child.

Dear Father, being Your child is worth more to me than any earthly thing. Is there something You'd like me to give up? Show me what it is, and I'll gladly let it go to please You. I love You with all my heart. Amen.

HE UNDERSTANDS

When Jesus heard that John had been killed,
He went from there by boat to a desert.
He wanted to be alone. When the people knew it,
they followed after Him by land from the cities.
MATTHEW 14:13

John was Jesus' cousin. Jesus loved John very much. He knew John had spent his life telling others about Jesus and preparing the way for Him. When Jesus learned John had died, He was very sad. Even Jesus, the Son of God, experienced sadness and heartbreak. During His time here on earth, Jesus felt the full spectrum of human emotion.

When we hurt, when we feel anxious or depressed, when we feel angry and frustrated, we can turn to Jesus. He's been there. He's felt the same emotions, and He cares about each of us. Even if you're not sure if your feelings are right, it's okay. Talk to Him. Listen to Him. He has compassion, and He understands.

Jesus, I am so thankful that You know what I'm feeling and that You understand. Amen.

WALKING ON WATER

Jesus said, "Come!" Peter got out of the boat and walked on the water to Jesus. But when he saw the strong wind, he was afraid. He began to go down in the water. He cried out, "Lord, save me!" At once Jesus put out His hand and took hold of him. Jesus said to Peter, "You have so little faith! Why did you doubt?"

MATTHEW 14:29–31

Even though Peter was in the middle of a storm, He heard Jesus' voice. He answered Jesus' call. Why would Peter step out of the safety of the boat into a stormy sea? He did it because that's where Jesus was. It's always safer to be in God's presence than out of it. Peter walked on the water as long as he kept his focus on Jesus. But when he let the wind and waves distract him, he started to drown. Jesus saved him, but He asked Peter, "Why did you lose faith? Why did you take your eyes off Me?"

When you hear Jesus calling you, obey Him. Keep your eyes on Him and trust Him to keep you safe.

Dear Father, help me keep my eyes on You even when other things compete for my attention. Amen.

EYE ON THE PRIZE

Peter took Jesus away from the others and spoke sharp words to Him. He said, "Never, Lord! This must not happen to You!" Then Jesus turned to Peter and said, "Get behind Me, Satan! You are standing in My way. You are not thinking how God thinks. You are thinking how man thinks."

MATTHEW 16:22–23

Jesus had just told His disciples about the bad things that would happen in the days to come. He told them how He'd suffer and be killed. Peter thought he was being a good friend to Jesus by saying, "I'll never let this happen to you!" But Peter didn't understand Jesus' purpose—that the whole reason Jesus came was to take the punishment for our sins.

It's important to keep your focus on God's purpose for your life. Don't get distracted by the way you want things to be right now. Instead, set your mind on the bigger picture of how God wants to use you to bring others to Him.

Dear Father, help me keep my eyes on You and Your purpose for my life. Amen.

HUMBLE

"Whoever is without pride as this little child is the greatest in the holy nation of heaven."
MATTHEW 18:4

Another way to say "without pride" is "humble." According to dictionary.com, the word *humble* means "not proud or arrogant; modest." It also means "courteously respectful." When a person is humble, she treats others like they're more important than she is, instead of demanding that others treat her like she's the most important.

In this passage, Jesus is saying that God prefers humility over arrogance. He likes it when we treat others like they are the important ones. He likes it when we depend on Him for everything. When we are humble toward God and others, God notices. He wants us to be like little children who respect their parents and depend on them for everything. He says that the most important, most honored people in heaven will be the ones who showed the most humility while on earth.

Dear Father, humility can be hard sometimes. Help me set aside my pride and self-importance and treat others with respect. Help me honor You by honoring the people around me. Make me like the little child You spoke of here, totally dependent on You. Amen.

HE'S BEEN THERE

He went on a little farther and got down with His face on the ground. He prayed, "My Father, if it can be done, take away what is before Me. Even so, not what I want but what You want." . . . He came and found them asleep again. Their eyes were heavy.

MATTHEW 26:39, 43

Jesus knew He didn't have much time. Soon He would be whipped, beaten, and nailed to a cross. He knew it would be a horrible, painful experience, and He was afraid. He asked God if there was any other way to offer salvation. Yet He told God, "Whatever You say, I'll do."

Jesus understands what it is to be afraid. He also understands loneliness. In that difficult time, He just wanted someone to stay awake with Him, to just be there for him, but all His friends fell asleep. When You feel alone and afraid, talk to Jesus. He's been there, and He understands.

Dear Jesus, thank You for going through such a hard thing for me. I know You died on the cross to take the punishment for my sins. Thank You for understanding every emotion I feel and for always being there no matter what. Amen.

GO AND TELL

"Go and make followers of all the nations. Baptize them in the name of the Father and of the Son and of the Holy Spirit. Teach them to do all the things I have told you. And I am with you always, even to the end of the world."

MATTHEW 28:19–20

These verses are known as the Great Commission. These were Jesus' last words, His last wishes. When someone speaks their last words, those words are often an important message for the listeners. He spoke to His disciples but also to all His followers who would ever live. That means us! His last words were, "Go. Tell others about Me because they need to hear. Teach them My ways. Lead them to Me so they can be My followers too. It's important."

Each day we must ask ourselves what we're doing to make disciples. Go—into your neighborhood, your school, your sports teams. Tell everyone how great God is. Teach them to follow Christ so they can have the joy and peace that come from being a Christian.

Dear Jesus, I want to honor Your last wishes. Show me ways to tell others about You.

BELIEF VS. RELATIONSHIP

When demons saw Him, they got down at His feet and cried out, "You are the Son of God!"

MARK 3:11

Many people say they believe in God. But believing in God and having a personal relationship with Him are two different things. We may believe the queen of England is a real person, but that doesn't mean we know her personally. This verse tells us that even the demons believe in God, and they know Jesus is His Son. Evil recognizes and fears the presence of God.

Don't be surprised when you're around people who don't know Christ and they feel uncomfortable around you. They may not like you, and they may not even know why. It's important to keep showing them Christ's love, kindness, patience, and compassion. When you display a consistent, loving attitude, they'll notice. Someday they may remember the difference Christ made in your life, and they'll want to know Him too.

Dear Jesus, it's hard to be around people who don't know You. Help me be consistent in living for You so they'll want to know You for themselves. Amen.

THE LITTLE THINGS

Jesus got into the boat. The man who had had the demons asked to go with Him. Jesus would not let him go but said to him, "Go home to your own people. Tell them what great things the Lord has done for you. Tell them how He had pity on you."

MARK 5:18–19

Jesus had a passing conversation with a man who needed Him. Jesus was in a hurry, but He made time to show compassion to this man. It was a little thing that made a big difference.

Many people want to do something *great* for God. But most of the time, the biggest impact happens on a small level. People are introduced to Christ because their friend talked to them about God. People want to become Christians because they see the difference Christ makes in the lives of people they know personally. They see kindness, generosity, and all the good characteristics God wants us to display in our lives. Don't worry about doing *great* things for God. Spend your time doing the *little* things for Him, and your life will make a big difference.

Dear Father, show me the small things I can do for You today. Amen.

HAPPY ENDING

At once he sent one of his soldiers and told him to bring the head of John the Baptist. The soldier went to the prison and cut off John's head. He took John's head in on a plate and gave it to the girl. The girl gave it to her mother. John's followers heard this. They went and took his body and buried it.

MARK 6:27–29

This account is hard to read. There's no question about it—John died a horrible death. Sometimes we get the mistaken idea that if we live for God, our lives will be easy. But John spent his life doing exactly what God called him to do. He was poor. Some people thought he was crazy. And in the end, he was killed for his belief. (Someone who dies for their faith is called a *martyr*.)

But no matter what difficult things we may experience here on earth, this isn't the end! Our time on earth is just chapter 1 of a never-ending story that for all Christians will have a very happy ending.

Dear Father, I know John is living out his happy ending with You. Remind me of this when I go through hard things. Amen.

COMPASSION

When Jesus got out of the boat, He saw many people gathered together. He had loving-pity for them. They were like sheep without a shepherd. He began to teach them many things.

Mark 6:34

Wherever Jesus went, crowds followed Him. They wanted His touch, His healing, and His wisdom. Even when He tried to get away and get some rest, they wouldn't leave Him alone. Yet He didn't get annoyed or frustrated. Instead, He had compassion on them. The word *compassion* means to feel sad with someone else and to try to help that person feel better. Jesus felt sad for the people who were hurting, and He wanted to help them.

As Christ's followers, we should feel compassion for those who are hurting, and we should try to help them. Next time you see someone who seems sad, think of something you can do to help them. When we show compassion, we imitate Christ, and God is pleased.

Dear Father, help me to help somebody today. Teach me to have compassion. Show me how to love them and make things better for them. Amen.

TELL EVERYBODY

They were very much surprised and wondered about [Jesus' healing of the man]. They said, "He has done all things well. He makes those who could not hear so they can hear. He makes those who could not speak so they can speak."

MARK 7:37

In this account, Jesus had just healed a man who was deaf and could not speak. Though He tried to do it in private, many people saw the healing take place. He asked them not to tell anyone because He knew some of the religious leaders were out to get Him. But the people couldn't help themselves. They were so amazed at how wonderful Jesus was, they had to tell everyone!

We should be just as amazed at the awesome things Christ does for us every day. We should tell everyone we know about His goodness so they can know Him too. Ask God for wisdom about who to share with and what to say. People need to hear the good news of Jesus Christ because He can change their lives for the better.

Dear Father, I want to tell everyone about how great Jesus is. Show me who to talk to and what to say.

PRACTICAL NEEDS

"I pity these people because they have been with Me three days and have nothing to eat."

MARK 8:2

In this account, Jesus fed four thousand people with seven loaves of bread and a few fish. He didn't perform this miracle just to show off. He did it because He felt compassion. He knew they were very hungry, but they stayed because they wanted to hear Him teach. Jesus met their practical needs because it was important. He could have just kept teaching in order to meet their spiritual needs. But Jesus cares about every part of us—body, soul, and spirit. God wants His children to have the same kind of compassion.

Do you know someone who has a practical need? Maybe they're lonely and you can offer friendship. Maybe they need something that you have plenty of and you can share what you have. Perhaps your mom or dad needs help cleaning the house or making dinner or doing some other chores. When we meet people's practical needs, we shine Christ's love on them.

Dear Father, show me how to love the people around me by meeting their practical needs. Amen.

SUCCESSFUL

"For what does a man have if he gets all the world and loses his own soul?"

MARK 8:36

Do you want to be successful? Most people do. Many people give up everything in order to have success. Some go deep into debt to go to an impressive college or university. Some work so many hours that they barely see their families. Some betray their friends to gain popularity. When they do these things, most people don't see them as bad. An education is a good thing, right? Parents work hard to provide for their families. And popularity—who doesn't want to be popular? That's not wrong, is it?

Success by the world's standards isn't the same as success by God's standards. Earthly success can steal our time, our years, our relationships, and our souls. But God's kind of success leads us to have healthy souls and spirits and to live rewarding, purpose-filled lives.

Dear Father, I don't want to get pulled into the trap of chasing earthly success. I want to live for You. Show me how to be successful in Your eyes. Amen.

THE COLT

He said to them, "Go into the town over there. As soon as you get there, you will find a young donkey tied. No man has ever sat on it. Let the donkey loose and bring it here."

MARK 11:2

Why would Jesus ask His disciples to get a young donkey that no one had ever sat on? That donkey was unbroken, untrained. Jesus planned to ride the animal, so why wouldn't He ask them to find a trained donkey? An unbroken colt would have trouble the first time it had a rider. It might buck or kick. In this case, it would be skittish because of the crowds, with people pushing and shouting and waving things in the air. Jesus knew this donkey didn't need to be trained because animals obey their masters. God created the colt, and the colt submitted to Jesus.

Sometimes God calls us to do something we feel unprepared for. Maybe we've never done it before. When that happens, we need to be like that colt. We need to submit, obey our Master, and give Him the glory.

Dear Father, I want to obey You like the colt obeyed Jesus. I'm Yours. I'll do whatever You ask. Amen.

PRETENDERS

Some people from the religious group who believe no one will be raised from the dead came to Jesus. They asked Him, "Teacher, Moses gave us a Law. It said, 'If a man's brother dies and leaves his wife behind, but no children, then his brother should marry his wife and raise children for his brother.' . . . When people are raised from the dead, whose wife will she be?"

Mark 12:18–19, 23

A *hypocrite* is a person who pretends to have moral or religious beliefs that they don't actually have. They are fakes. Why did these people pretend to care about whose wife this woman would be if they didn't even believe people would be raised from the dead? They were trying to trick Jesus.

It's important never to trick people in a mean way or try to set them up to get in trouble. That's dishonest, and it doesn't please God. We should always be honest and straightforward with everyone. It's better not to say anything than to pretend something that isn't true.

Dear Father, I don't want to be a hypocrite. Help me always to be sincere in my words and actions. Amen.

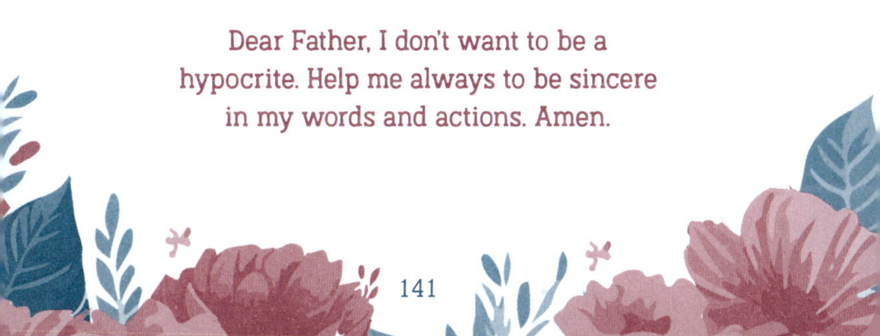

SELF-RIGHTEOUS

Jesus taught them, saying, "Look out for the teachers of the Law. They like to walk around in long coats. They like to have the respect of men as they stand in the center of town where people gather. They like to have the important seats in the places of worship and the important places at big suppers. They take houses from poor women whose husbands have died. They cover up the bad they do by saying long prayers. They will be punished all the more."

MARK 12:38–40

In this passage, Jesus described people who tried to look good on the outside but on the inside were unkind and had no compassion. These people were self-righteous, which means they thought they were godly, but they weren't. These people wore nice clothes and said long, fancy prayers so everyone could hear. But when no one was watching, they took advantage of the poor.

God loves truly righteous people, but He can't stand those who are self-righteous. We should always seek to impress God, not other people.

Dear Father, forgive me for times when I've tried to impress others instead of trying to impress You. Change my heart, and make me truly righteous. Amen.

LOOK UP!

They said to themselves, "Who will roll the stone away from the door of the grave for us?" But when they looked, they saw the very large stone had been rolled away.

MARK 16:3–4

After Jesus died, His body was placed in a tomb, or a cave. A boulder was placed in front of the opening to keep anyone from going in, and two soldiers guarded the tomb. A group of women brought spices to put on Jesus' body. They worried about how they would move the stone out of the way so they could care for Jesus' body. But when they looked up, the stone was already rolled away!

Sometimes we worry about what seems like an impossible task. But God tells us we shouldn't worry about anything. Instead, we should look up—look to God. Nothing is impossible for Him, and He will always take care of us. In this case, Jesus was alive! He didn't need those spices. God loves to surprise us with the very things we thought were impossible.

Dear Father, thank You for raising Jesus from the dead. Thank You for all the great things You've done for me. When I worry, remind me to look up! Amen.

LIFT YOUR HEAD!

"Go and tell His followers and Peter that He is going ahead of you into Galilee. You will see Him there as He told you."

Mark 16:7

An angel spoke to the women at the tomb. He told them to tell the disciples and Peter what they'd seen. The disciples were together in a group, but Peter was off by himself. Before Jesus died, Peter promised to stand by Jesus. But when things got really bad, Peter denied even knowing Jesus. He felt embarrassed and ashamed that he didn't keep his word. But Jesus takes away our shame! Psalm 3:3 says He is the lifter of our heads.

Don't ever let shame or embarrassment about past mistakes keep you from being with your friends, especially if they're Christians. We need our friends. It's important to admit when we're wrong, but our true friends will recognize that we've all messed up at times. Apologize if needed, and leave the past in the past. Jesus has taken our shame, so we don't need to carry it with us.

Dear Father, sometimes I feel ashamed or embarrassed about something I've done. Thank You for taking away my shame. Help me hold up my head. Amen.

PEACE ON EARTH

"Greatness and honor to our God in the highest heaven and peace on earth among men who please Him."

LUKE 2:14

Luke told the story of Jesus' birth in a beautiful way. When the angels appeared to the shepherds, they said the words above. Many Christmas cards don't finish the verse. They say, "Peace on earth," which is a lovely thought. However, the verse actually says, "Peace on earth among men who please Him."

God's promises are for those who please Him, not for those who disrespect Him and ignore His laws. He wants everyone to love Him. He blesses everyone at times, even if they don't honor Him. But the promises of salvation and heaven, of a sense of peace and joy in our hearts—those are special blessings reserved for those who choose to love Him. If you've made the choice to love Jesus and follow Him, His peace is right there for you. Whenever you feel anxious or upset, you need only to go to God. He will give you His peace.

Dear Father, thank You for Your promise of peace. I love You and want to please You. Amen.

WHO IS HE?

Jesus said to them, "But who do you say that I am?" Peter said, "You are the Christ of God."

LUKE 9:20

Jesus asked His closest friends, "Who do you say that I am?" Peter answered correctly. Jesus' question isn't just for the disciples. He asks each of us the same question. Do we truly believe Jesus is God's Son? Do we believe He died for our sins and that God raised Him from the dead? Do we believe He's the King of kings and Lord of lords and has power over everything?

If we really, truly believe that, why do we worry about anything? What is the worst that could happen to us? With Christ on our side, we can relax. Fear and anxiety have no place in the lives of those who truly believe.

Dear Jesus, I believe You are God's Son. I believe You died on the cross for my sins and You rose again on the third day. I believe You have power over everything in my life. But sometimes I struggle with fear. I worry about things. Teach me to have faith in You. Help me understand You better so I won't be afraid. Amen.

THE HELPER

"When they take you to the places of worship and to the courts and to the leaders of the country, do not be worried about what you should say or how to say it. The Holy Spirit will tell you what you should say at that time."

LUKE 12:11–12

Have you ever been in a difficult situation where you didn't know what to say or do? Jesus said that would happen. In this passage, He was warning His disciples that there might be a time when they'd be punished for being Christians. When we enter a situation with a spirit of prayer, the Holy Spirit takes over. He puts thoughts in our minds that we wouldn't have thought on our own. He gives us words to say that we couldn't have prepared in advance—but they're just the right words. When we go through our days with a spirit of prayer and a sense of leaning on the Holy Spirit, He guides us and shows us what to do.

Dear Father, thank You for sending Your Holy Spirit to show me what to do and give me words to say. Amen.

WHERE YOUR TREASURE IS

Zaccheus stood up and said to the Lord, "Lord, see! Half of what I own I will give to poor people. And if I have taken money from anyone in a wrong way, I will pay him back four times as much." Jesus said to him, "Today, a person has been saved in this house. This man is a Jew also."

LUKE 19:8–9

Zaccheus was a tax collector. In Bible times, tax collectors had a reputation for cheating people. They took too much money, gave some to the government, and kept the rest. But when Zaccheus met Jesus, his life was changed. He now wanted to use his money in a way that would please God.

In Matthew 6:21 we're told that where our treasure is, that's where our hearts can be found. Zaccheus showed that his heart was sincere because he cared more about pleasing God, helping the poor, and making things right with people he'd cheated than about getting rich. We can find out where our hearts are by looking at what's important to us.

Dear Father, You are my treasure.
More than anything, I want to please You. Amen.

NOT OF GOD

They watched Jesus and they sent men who pretended to be good people to watch Him. They wanted to trap Him in something He said. Then they could give Him over to the leader of the people who had the right and the power to say what to do with Him.

LUKE 20:20

The religious people did not like Jesus. They thought that when God sent a Savior, He would be a mighty earthly king. They wanted a king who would make Israel powerful, but Jesus was a different kind of king. Because they didn't like Him, they made secret plans against Him. They whispered and gossiped about Him. They tried to trick Him and trap Him so they could punish Him.

God doesn't work that way—in whispers and gossip and secret plans. When we realize we're in the middle of that kind of behavior, we should leave as soon as possible. Those things are not of God.

Dear Father, it's easy to get pulled into gossip and mean-girl behavior. But that's not who I want to be. Help me stay away from all that. I only want to reflect Your love. Amen.

MAKING FUN

Then Herod and his soldiers were very bad to Jesus and made fun of Him. They put a beautiful coat on Him and sent Him back to Pilate.

LUKE 23:11

Have you ever been made fun of? It happens to everyone at one time or another. When someone makes fun of us in a mean way, it's called being mocked. It feels terrible. Because Jesus said He was God's Son, the soldiers made Him wear a king's robe and a crown of thorns, all while they beat Him up and spat on Him.

If you're ever made fun of, remember that Jesus knows what it feels like. He sees you, and He cares. If you ever see someone else being made fun of, do what you can to make the behavior stop. When others are being mean to someone, you can show God's love by seeing that person and showing you care.

Dear Father, help me to stand with people who are hurting. Even though it's hard to stand against bullies and mean people, give me courage to always do what's right. Amen.

ABIDE

"Get your life from Me and I will live in you. No branch can give fruit by itself. It has to get life from the vine. You are able to give fruit only when you have life from Me. I am the Vine and you are the branches. Get your life from Me. Then I will live in you and you will give much fruit. You can do nothing without Me."

JOHN 15:4–5

Another translation of verse 4 says, "Abide in me as I abide in you" (NRSV). To abide means to remain or to stay. When we stay in Christ, He gives us life. When we remain in Him, He chooses to live in us. He compares our relationship with Him to a healthy vine with branches of fruit. As long as the branches remain attached to the healthy vine, they will produce fruit. But if a branch separates from the vine, it will dry up and die.

When we remain in Christ, He gives us life, and good "fruit" will grow from that healthy relationship. But when we walk away from Christ, we walk away from our life source.

Dear Jesus, thank You for being my life source. I want to remain in You. Amen.

STOP FIGHTING

Then Jesus said to Peter, "Put your sword back where it belongs. Am I not to go through what My Father has given Me to go through?"

JOHN 18:11

When people tried to arrest Jesus, Peter drew a sword. Peter was ready to fight for his friend. But Jesus stopped Peter. Jesus knew He needed to go through some hard things in order to live out God's purpose for His life. He also knew God would fight His battles for Him.

When life puts us in difficult circumstances, it's normal to want to fight against them. But God wants us to relax and let Him fight our battles for us. We may need to go through some hard things to prepare us for His plan for our lives. We can trust that our loving heavenly Father will take care of us.

Dear Father, when things don't go the way I want them to, I can be like Peter. I want to get out a sword and fight somebody! Remind me to trust You. I know You love me and have a special plan for my life. Help me endure difficult things with faith that You're in control. Amen.

RESPECT AUTHORITY

Pilate said, "Will You not speak to me? Do You not know that I have the right and the power to nail You to a cross? I have the right and the power to let You go free also." Jesus said, "You would not have any right or power over Me if it were not given you from above. For this reason the one who handed Me over to you has the worse sin."

JOHN 19:10–11

Pilate was the governor of Judea, and he had a lot of power. He would make the decision to crucify Jesus or let Him go free. He asked Jesus some questions, but Jesus remained quiet. When Pilate pressed Him for an answer, Jesus said, "God is the one who gave you the power you have."

This is a good reminder that we should respect those in authority over us because God is the one who controls who is placed in what positions. Even if we disagree with an authority figure, we can trust that God is using all things to bring about His perfect plan.

Dear Father, help me respect my teachers and leaders even if I disagree with them. I know You are in control. Amen.

CHRISTIANS ARE EVERYWHERE

Joseph was from the town of Arimathea. He was a follower of Jesus but was afraid of the Jews. So he worshiped without anyone knowing it. He asked Pilate if he could take away the body of Jesus. Pilate said he could. Then Joseph came and took it away. Nicodemus came also. The first time he had come to Jesus had been at night. He brought with him a large box of spices.

JOHN 19:38–39

Joseph and Nicodemus were like secret-agent Christians. They followed Jesus, but they didn't let everyone know. They weren't ashamed of Jesus; they just knew that sometimes it's best to remain quiet. But when Jesus died, they weren't afraid to step forward. They took Jesus' body and buried Him with honor.

Christ followers are everywhere! When we feel alone, when we feel like no one understands our faith in Christ, we can ask God to show us other believers. They are there. They may just be the quiet ones. When the time is right, God will nudge them to step forward.

Dear Father, I need Christian friends.
Please show me others who love You. Amen.

JESUS TALKED ABOUT US

Jesus said to him, "Thomas, because you have seen Me, you believe. Those are happy who have never seen Me and yet believe!"

JOHN 20:29

Thomas earned the nickname "Doubting Thomas" because when Jesus rose from the dead and appeared to His disciples, Thomas didn't really believe it was Jesus. He wanted proof. Jesus showed Thomas the scars on His hands and feet, and Thomas finally believed. Jesus said, "You believe because you have proof. Blessed are those who believe without this kind of proof." Jesus was talking about us!

Way back in Bible times, two thousand years ago, Jesus knew we would live, and He knew we would believe. Because of our faith, we are blessed. When we struggle to have faith, when we struggle to believe God's promises, we can remember this. Jesus saw us. He knew us already. And He blessed us with His inner peace and joy.

Dear Jesus, thank You for Your special blessing on my life. I'm excited for the day I'll see You face-to-face. Until then, I believe and I love You with all my heart. Amen.

WATCHING FOR JESUS

Early in the morning Jesus stood on the shore of the lake. The followers did not know it was Jesus.

JOHN 21:4

Jesus was supposed to be dead. Many of His followers watched Him die. So when they saw this man on the shore, they didn't give Him a second look. They had no idea it was Jesus. He could have done some showy miracle to get everyone's attention, but He didn't. He just stood there, quietly watching. After a while, He spoke to them, and they still didn't recognize Him right away. They were fishing, and Jesus told them where to cast their nets. When they did, they hauled in 153 fish! That's when Peter recognized Jesus. He jumped out of the boat and swam to Him.

The Lord doesn't always show Himself in obvious ways. Sometimes He shows up quietly in unexpected places. It's important to always be on the lookout for where God is working. We may be surprised at where He appears.

Dear Father, help me to always watch for where You're at work. I want to join You there. Amen.

GIVING WHAT WE CAN

The Christians agreed that each one should give what money he could to help the Christians living in Judea. They did this and sent it to the church leaders with Barnabas and Saul.

ACTS 11:29–30

The early Christians had to scatter because it wasn't safe for them to stay in one place. A group of Christians learned there was a severe famine in Judea where some other Christians lived. They all gave what they could and sent it to those Christians. They didn't just say, "I'll pray for them," though prayer is always good. They didn't give advice. They actually gave their hard-earned money.

God didn't give us our resources so we could keep them to ourselves or spend them only on our pleasure. He blesses us with money and other things so we can share with those in need. Talk to your parents, and ask God to show you what you can share with others who need what you have.

Dear Father, I want to be like those early Christians. I know there are people who need what I have. Show me what You'd like me to give. Amen.

ACCEPTED

When they read it, they were glad for the comfort and strength it brought them. Judas and Silas were preachers also. They preached to the Christians and helped them to become stronger in the faith.

ACTS 15:31–32

In this passage, some Gentile Christians (Christians who were not Jews) read a letter that contained some good news. A church council of Jewish Christians had been arguing that the Gentiles had to follow all the old Jewish rules to be accepted in the church. The Gentiles were worried they would not be accepted as Christians because they didn't have the right background. But the church council prayed and talked with one another. They listened to the Holy Spirit. They finally decided it was silly to expect everyone to be the same. We're all different! The Gentiles were relieved to hear they'd be accepted. God opens His arms to everyone, no matter their background.

Do you know someone who is an outsider? Treat them with God's kindness, and show them they're accepted, wanted, and loved.

Dear Father, thank You for wanting me and accepting me. Help me reach out to others with the same kind of love.

TRANSFORMED

Do not act like the sinful people of the world. Let God change your life. First of all, let Him give you a new mind. Then you will know what God wants you to do. And the things you do will be good and pleasing and perfect.

ROMANS 12:2

To be conformed to something means to take on its shape. Water conforms to the shape of a glass, and play dough conforms to the shape of its container. To be transformed means to change into something new and different. Both words have the word *form* as the root.

A form is a shape. God doesn't want His children to be conformed to, or shaped like, the world. Instead, He wants to transform us, to change us into an entirely new shape! He wants to make something new and different and beautiful of our lives. Who wants to be like everybody else when God wants to make us beautiful, unique butterflies? His transformation takes place as we fill our minds with His Word.

Dear Father, I don't want to be like everyone else. I want to be exactly who You created me to be. Amen.

DON'T JUDGE

Who are you to tell another person's servant if he is right or wrong? It is to his owner that he does good or bad. The Lord is able to help him.

ROMANS 14:4

God doesn't want us to judge other people. It's His job to judge. It's our job to love. However, when He says not to judge, He doesn't mean we're supposed to accept sin. There are some laws that God has stated clearly in His Word, such as "Don't kill people" and "Don't steal." When we enforce those laws, we're not judging. We're simply enforcing what God has already judged to be right and wrong.

But there are some gray areas that aren't directly addressed in the Bible. In those areas, we're to act the way the Holy Spirit leads us to behave. But if someone chooses to behave differently, we're supposed to love them, show kindness, and ask God to show them what's right. But we're never supposed to put ourselves in God's place.

Dear Father, help me to remember my place. I know I'm supposed to love others, not judge them. Give me wisdom to know right from wrong, and help me love those I disagree with.

PUFFED UP OR BUILT UP?

But love makes one strong. The person who thinks he knows all the answers still has a lot to learn. But if he loves God, he is known by God also.

1 CORINTHIANS 8:1–3

"Knowledge puffs up, but love builds up" (NRSV). That's the way another translation of the Bible words 1 Corinthians 8:1, and it's kind of catchy. It's short and easy to remember. When we think we know more than others, or when we think we're always right, our egos get puffed up. We start to think we're better than other people.

That's not how God wants us to think. Love treats others like *they're* the important ones. Love builds up other people, encourages them, and makes them feel great. When we're more concerned about being right than about loving others, we have a lot to learn. But when love is our most important goal, God notices, and He is pleased.

Dear Father, forgive me for the times I've wanted to have the final say. Help me put others first. Help me to encourage others and build them up. Teach me to love like You love.

THE LORD'S SUPPER

When He had given thanks, He broke it and said, "Take this bread and eat it. This is My body which is broken for you. Do this to remember Me."

1 Corinthians 11:24

When Paul wrote this letter to the Corinthians, he had to get after them about some bad things they were doing. One thing that disappointed Paul was that they didn't take the Lord's Supper seriously. They treated it like a party instead of a solemn occasion. They used the Lord's Supper event as an excuse to eat and drink too much, and they didn't think much about the reason behind it.

The Lord's Supper is not a meal we eat to get full. It's something we do to think about and remember what Jesus did for us when He died on the cross. His body (the bread) was beaten, bruised, and broken. His blood (the wine or grape juice) was shed. He suffered terrible pain so we wouldn't have to. He paid the heavy price for our sins because He knew we couldn't pay it for ourselves.

Dear Jesus, thank You for what You did for me on the cross. Amen.

THE ANSWER IS YES

Jesus says yes to all of God's many promises. It is through Jesus that we say, "Let it be so," when we give thanks to God.

2 CORINTHIANS 1:20

Sometimes circumstances prevent us from keeping our promises. We feel bad, but there's nothing we can do to change things. Some people make promises—even though they know they can't keep them—in order to get what they want. But when God makes a promise, He always keeps it. When we remind God of any of His promises, His answer is always "Yes!"

So why don't we take advantage of His promises more than we do? For many of us, the problem is that we don't know His promises. We might say, "God, You promised to give me peace during difficult times, but I don't feel peace right now. Can you deliver some peace, please?"—but we'd never know to ask for peace if we didn't know He promised it. We learn about God's many promises by reading His Word. Keep a list of God's promises in a notebook or journal. You can cash in those promises anytime, and God will say yes.

Dear Father, thank You for keeping all Your promises. Amen.

A CHEERFUL GIVER

Each man should give as he has decided in his heart. He should not give, wishing he could keep it. Or he should not give if he feels he has to give. God loves a man who gives because he wants to give.

2 CORINTHIANS 9:7

Have you ever shared something with your sibling, cousin, or friend because you were told to? You may have done the right thing, but in your heart you resented it. We've all done that. But God is more generous than we can imagine, and He loves giving us things! He gives even to the point of pain. After all, He gave His Son so we could be saved. It hurt Him to watch His Son die, but He did it gladly because He loves us.

We're made in God's image, which means we're created to be generous. God wants us to give what we have to help others, and He wants us to give with excitement. God loves a cheerful giver.

Dear Father, help me find joy in giving. Show me what I can give to You and others. Whether it's time, money, or something else, help me give cheerfully. Amen.

LIVE IN PEACE

Last of all, Christian brothers, good-bye. Do that which makes you complete. Be comforted. Work to get along with others. Live in peace. The God of love and peace will be with you.

2 CORINTHIANS 13:11

As Paul ended his second letter to the church at Corinth, he tagged on a few last words of wisdom. When he said, "Do what makes you complete," he meant he wanted them to live in unity. He didn't want them to be divided. He repeated his message by telling them to get along with each other and live in peace.

God loves peace. He wants us to do our best to get along with others. We don't have to agree with everyone about everything—that would be boring! We each have different personalities and preferences. But as much as possible, we should respect each other, be kind, and try to live in peace even with those with whom we disagree.

Dear Father, I want to be a peaceful person. Sometimes I'm disappointed or upset when others don't agree with me. Help me respond in a pleasant way and with kindness. Help me live in peace with those around me. Amen.

WALK WITH THE SPIRIT

I say this to you: Let the Holy Spirit lead you in each step. Then you will not please your sinful old selves. The things our old selves want to do are against what the Holy Spirit wants. The Holy Spirit does not agree with what our sinful old selves want. These two are against each other. So you cannot do what you want to do.

GALATIANS 5:16–17

Each of us is born with a human nature that leans toward sin. Left on our own, we are mostly selfish and self-centered. We want what we want. As long as *we're* happy, we don't care if others get what they want.

Most parents try to teach their children to think of others, but living the way God wants us to live doesn't come naturally. So how do we overcome that sin nature? We do it by walking with the Holy Spirit. When we travel through each day with Him, talking to Him, praising Him, and listening to Him, we become more like Him.

Dear Father, thank You for sending Your Holy Spirit to walk with me. Make me more like You each day. Amen.

ROOTS AND FRUIT

But the fruit that comes from having the Holy Spirit in our lives is: love, joy, peace, not giving up, being kind, being good, having faith, being gentle, and being the boss over our own desires. The Law is not against these things.

GALATIANS 5:22–23

These are fun verses to read. They paint a pretty picture of fruit on the vine. That fruit occurs naturally when a vine has healthy roots. Many people read these verses and want to focus on the fruit instead of the roots. But if the roots aren't healthy, there will be no fruit.

Are you impatient? Walk with the Holy Spirit. Unkind? Focus on spending more time with God. The Holy Spirit produces the fruit. We can't produce it on our own. If we want more fruit or healthier fruit, we must walk in the Spirit.

Dear Father, I've often tried to produce the fruits of love, joy, patience, and kindness on my own. I've tried really hard to have self-control. Now I understand that those qualities will occur naturally the more time I spend with You. Walk with me, talk with me, and remind me of Your constant presence in my life. Amen.

YOU ARE IMPORTANT

We are His work. He has made us to belong to Christ Jesus so we can work for Him. He planned that we should do this.

EPHESIANS 2:10

God spent time making you. He thought you up and planned every detail. He decided what color your hair and eyes would be. He planned each freckle, each birthmark. He chose your personality, your gifts and talents. He chose everything about you. Nothing about you was an accident.

Though we may not like everything about ourselves, we can be confident that God made each of us with a purpose, to complete specific good works. He placed us in a certain time and place so we can fill parts of a great puzzle. Look around. What can you do to show God's love to those around you? If you don't do it, it may not get done. What can you do to prepare for the work He has for you in the future? Study hard. Develop your skills and your character. You are important to God's work!

Dear Father, show me what You need me to do today. I want to complete the work You've planned for me. Amen.

DOING GOD'S WORK

Christ gave gifts to men. He gave to some the gift to be missionaries, some to be preachers, others to be preachers who go from town to town. He gave others the gift to be church leaders and teachers. These gifts help His people work well for Him. And then the church which is the body of Christ will be made strong.

EPHESIANS 4:11–12

Many people mistakenly believe that God's work is only for the people who get paid to be in the ministry. That's not true! God gives some people special gifts and talents and calls them to specific work. These people are missionaries, preachers, evangelists, church leaders, and teachers. But all these people are there to help the rest of us do God's work. The preachers and teachers teach us about God so we can "work well for Him." We're not supposed to take in their teaching just for ourselves. A preacher's job is to equip the rest of us to do ministry. No matter our jobs or our place in the world, we *all* are called to do God's work every day.

Dear Father, show me the work You have for me today, and help me to complete it well. Amen.

LIFE GOALS

I want to know Him. I want to have the same power in my life that raised Jesus from the dead. I want to understand and have a share in His sufferings and be like Christ in His death.

PHILIPPIANS 3:10

This verse is filled with powerful life goals. First, Paul wrote that he wanted to know God. He didn't mean a head knowledge, like memorizing facts for a test. He was talking about a super-close, heart-to-heart, best-friend kind of knowing. Next, Paul wanted to experience God's power in his life.

If we're Christians, Christ lives in us. If we say we know Him but we don't see His power working in our lives, something is wrong. One of the greatest ways He shows His power is by helping us say no to sin. Finally, Paul wanted to be like Christ. These were Paul's life goals, and they're pretty good goals for the rest of us too.

Dear Father, I have the same life goals as Paul. I want to know You. I want us to be best friends! I want to see Your power in my life. Finally, I want to become more and more like You every day. Amen.

THINK ABOUT. . .

Christian brothers, keep your minds thinking about whatever is true, whatever is respected, whatever is right, whatever is pure, whatever can be loved, and whatever is well thought of. If there is anything good and worth giving thanks for, think about these things. Keep on doing all the things you learned and received and heard from me. Do the things you saw me do. Then the God Who gives peace will be with you.

PHILIPPIANS 4:8–9

In today's world, modern technology competes for our attention. Sometimes other people fill our thoughts. If something bothers us, someone hurts our feelings, or we're worried about a test at school, that's all we can think about. It takes discipline to push those negative thoughts to the side and focus on the good things God wants us to think about. But when we make the effort, we feel so much better! Try to focus your mind on good, pure, lovely, God-honoring thoughts today.

Dear Father, I can't always control the thoughts that show up in my mind. But with Your help, I can control the ones that stay there. Help me focus on things that honor You today. Amen.

NAILED TO THE CROSS

When you were dead in your sins, you were not set free from the sinful things of the world. But God forgave your sins and gave you new life through Christ. We had broken the Law many ways. Those sins were held against us by the Law. That Law had writings which said we were sinners. But now He has destroyed that writing by nailing it to the cross.

COLOSSIANS 2:13–14

The Bible says in Romans 6:23 that the wages for our sin is death. Wages are something we earn. When we complete a job, the boss gives us our wages. They are ours—we've worked for them and we deserve them. By saying the wages of our sin is death, Paul means we deserve death because of our sin. All that sin was written down like a bill that needed to be paid. When Jesus died, He took that bill and nailed it to the cross! He said, "Look, Satan. This is what they earned, and I'm here to pay it." When we accept Christ's gift, we don't have to pay that bill. Christ paid it for us.

Dear Jesus, thank You for paying the bill for my sin. Amen.

SPEAK LOVE

Speak with them in such a way they will want to listen to you. Do not let your talk sound foolish. Know how to give the right answer to anyone.

COLOSSIANS 4:6

Our most important job here on earth is to tell others about Jesus. We tell with our actions by living in a way that honors God, being kind, and showing love. But we also tell with our words. When we speak to others in a way that makes them think we don't like them or approve of their actions, people often get defensive and won't listen to us. But when we season our words with love, kindness, and compassion, others feel comfortable. When we talk to them in a way that makes them feel cared for and accepted, they are drawn to us. Then they're more likely to listen when we talk about Jesus. Make it a habit to think before you speak and to talk in a way that shows grace, kindness, and love.

Dear Father, help me speak in a way that honors You and shows Your love to others. Amen.

FULL OF JOY

Be full of joy all the time. Never stop praying. In everything give thanks. This is what God wants you to do because of Christ Jesus.

1 THESSALONIANS 5:16–18

Paul wanted believers to be full of joy all the time. How is that possible? We can't control our circumstances, and some situations are not joyful! So Paul coached us in how to remain joyful. We should never stop praying, and we should give thanks in everything. All day long, from the moment we wake up until we fall asleep, we should include the Holy Spirit in our thoughts. God wants us to talk to Him, out loud or in our minds, about everything we do. Whether through formal prayer or casual conversations while we're doing other things, God wants us to keep talking to Him. And no matter what happens, we should find things to thank God for.

There's always something to be grateful for. When we do these two things, we'll be able to face everything with an inner joy and peace.

Dear Father, thank You for staying with me so I can talk to You all the time. I'm so grateful for Your presence in my life. Show me what true joy looks like. Amen.

ABOUT WORK

If a man does not work, he should not eat. We hear that some are not working. But they are spending their time trying to see what others are doing. Our words to such people are that they should be quiet and go to work. They should eat their own food. In the name of the Lord Jesus Christ we say this.

2 THESSALONIANS 3:10–12

In early Bible times, God told farmers that when they gathered wheat from their fields, they should leave the corners alone so those who didn't have enough food could gather some. God provided food for the poor, but He didn't bundle it up and hand it to them. They still had to get up, go to a field, and gather it for themselves.

God knows that work is good for us. It makes us tired so we'll sleep better. It builds our sense of self-worth. And it helps us earn others' respect. God doesn't want us to be busybodies—people who don't really work but spend their time talking about other people's business. Instead, He wants us to stay busy and productive. Work is good for our spirits.

Dear Father, teach me to be a hard worker. Amen.

DON'T STOP!

But you, Christian brothers, do not get tired of doing good.

2 THESSALONIANS 3:13

Have you ever gotten tired of doing the right thing? Maybe you grow weary of doing the dishes because you know they'll just get dirty again after the next meal. Or maybe it's hard to keep being nice to that person who isn't nice to you. Whatever the reason, it's important to keep doing the right thing every time. When others see our consistency in doing good, they'll be curious about what makes us different. Our reliable good deeds draw others to Him. Our steadiness provides comfort and stability in a world that can feel chaotic.

Next time you're tempted to ignore the obvious good deed that needs to be done, remember that you're making a difference. God sees, He knows, and He's thrilled when His children do good things.

Dear Father, sometimes I feel like I'm the only one who cares about doing the right thing. Remind me that I'm making good choices and doing good deeds because those choices really do make this world a better place. Amen.

THE LOVE OF MONEY

The love of money is the beginning of all kinds of sin. Some people have turned from the faith because of their love for money. They have made much pain for themselves because of this.

1 TIMOTHY 6:10

The love of money leads to all kinds of bad things. But many people misread this verse and believe that money itself is bad. Money isn't alive. It's just a thing. Money can't make good or bad decisions. Money isn't sinful, but the *love* of money is. When we work hard, God sometimes rewards us with money. Money is nice to have. It helps us get the things we need. It allows us to help other people. Money can bring about some amazing things for God's kingdom. But when we love money more than we love God, our behavior reflects that. We start thinking about how we can get more money or more stuff, and we stop caring about how to please God. When you earn money of your own, always remember that it's a tool to use for God's purposes.

Dear Father, help me have the right attitude about money. Amen.

A GOOD FRIEND

Onesiphorus was not ashamed of me in prison. He came often to comfort me. May the Lord show loving-kindness to his family. When he came to Rome, he looked everywhere until he found me. You know what a help he was to me in Ephesus. When the Lord comes again, may He show loving-kindness to Onesiphorus.

2 TIMOTHY 1:16–18

Paul went through some really hard times. He was put in jail because people wanted him to stop telling others about Jesus. During those hard times, Paul had some loyal friends who made his life easier. Back then prisoners didn't eat unless a friend or family member brought them food. They might freeze unless someone brought them a blanket. Paul's friend Onesiphorus was that kind of friend. He looked for Paul—remember, there were no phones or text messages back then. He helped Paul and encouraged him.

When someone goes through a hard time, it's easy to forget about them as we take care of our own lives. But we should strive to be loyal friends. We should look for ways to encourage and help the people around us.

Dear Father, make me a good, loyal, encouraging friend to others. Amen.

KINDNESS AND GRACE

Yes, Christian brother, I want you to be of use to me as a Christian. Give my heart new joy in Christ.

PHILEMON 20

Paul's letter to Philemon tells an interesting story. A man named Onesimus was an escaped slave. After he escaped, he became a Christian. His former owner, Philemon, was also a Christian. Paul helped Onesimus understand that he needed to make things right with Philemon. He encouraged him to return to Philemon and talk things through. But Philemon could have punished Onesimus severely! Paul wrote a letter to Philemon explaining that Onesimus wanted to make things right. He asked Philemon not to punish Onesimus but to show grace. Paul said it would refresh his heart if Philemon showed kindness to Onesimus. By doing the right thing, Philemon would bring Paul joy during a difficult time.

When we show kindness and grace to others, it blesses the person we're kind to. But it also blesses those around us by creating a peaceful environment.

Dear Father, make me a blessing to others. Help me show kindness and grace even to those who have wronged me. Amen.

HARD TIMES

Because Jesus was tempted as we are and suffered as we do, He understands us and He is able to help us when we are tempted.

HEBREWS 2:18

When Jesus lived on earth, He experienced all the common things any human experiences. He laughed. He cried. He felt the warmth of friendship. He felt the sting of rejection. He felt hurt when His friends betrayed Him. He cried when someone He loved died. Because He experienced all those things, He is able to help us when we struggle with the same kinds of things.

When we go through difficult times, we may question God's purpose. Why would a loving God let us suffer? But when we experience hard things, we become more compassionate. We're able to help others through their suffering because we've been there and we understand. Next time you go through something hard, remember that God never wastes our experiences. If we let Him, He will use those difficult times to make us more like Him.

Dear Father, I don't want to go through difficult times. When I go through something hard, remind me that one day You'll use my experience to help someone else.

WHO YOU ARE

Do not throw away your trust, for your reward will be great.

HEBREWS 10:35

Another word for *trust* is *confidence*. Don't throw away your confidence in Christ. We should always have confidence in who we are in Him—a cherished daughter of the King of kings. Satan tries to tear down our confidence by telling us lies. Those lies are different for everyone, based on our personalities and weaknesses. But they all hold the same message. Satan tries to convince us that we're not enough: not good enough, not smart enough, not pretty enough, not *whatever* enough.

Anytime we doubt ourselves or feel we don't measure up, we can remember who we are. We are royalty! A princess's value doesn't lie in her own abilities or talents. It lies in who her parents are. She's of royal lineage, and that alone gives her immense value. As God's children, we never need to doubt our worth. Have confidence in your place in God's family. Hold your head high and remember who you are.

Dear Father, thank You for making me Your daughter. When I doubt myself, remind me of who I am. Amen.

FOLLOWING ORDERS

This letter is from James. I am a servant owned by God and the Lord Jesus Christ. I greet the twelve family groups of the Jewish nation living in many parts of the world.

JAMES 1:1

What does it mean to be a servant? If a person is a servant, it means someone else is the boss. It means someone else is calling the shots. It's the servant's job to do whatever the boss says. It would be disrespectful for a servant to question her master. The servant is simply to carry out the orders.

Like James, we are servants, owned by God and the Lord Jesus. Our job is to carry out His orders. The most important duty of a servant of God is to love. We're to love God with our whole hearts. We're to love others as we love ourselves. We're to be humble. We're to do good works in order to show God's love in this world. We're to include Him in all our thoughts, actions, and conversations. When we obey His commands to the best of our ability, we honor our Master.

Dear Father, I am Your servant. I want to honor You. Amen.

TESTS

My Christian brothers, you should be happy when you have all kinds of tests. You know these prove your faith. It helps you not to give up.

James 1:2–3

The word *test* has a bad vibe. When we think of a test, we think of spelling lists and history facts and long, difficult math equations. Those rarely bring happiness. James didn't mean we should be silly-happy when hard things happen. But he wanted us to view those difficulties, or tests, as opportunities to grow in our faith. They give us the chance to prove we believe what we *say* we believe.

We say that God will take care of us no matter what. Do we still feel that way when we face the school bully? We say we can do all things through Christ who gives us strength. What about when we have to give a speech at school and we have stage fright? We say God is good. What about when our parents get divorced? Hard times, faced with faith, give us the chance to grow into the strong, confident young women God created us to be.

Dear Father, help me see the opportunities in the middle of hard times. Amen.

WORD EDITOR

If a person thinks he is religious, but does not keep his tongue from speaking bad things, he is fooling himself. His religion is worth nothing.

James 1:26

Later in his book, James compared the tongue to a ship's rudder. The rudder is very small, but it directs huge ships. He also compared the tongue to a tiny spark. It may be small, but it can start a wildfire that soon burns out of control and destroys everything in its path.

God wants His children to control their tongues. That means we must learn to edit our words before they come out of our mouths. Once we say something, whether it's foul language, a mean comment, or hurtful gossip, we can't take it back. We may apologize, but the person will still remember the hurt they felt when the words were spoken. As God's daughters, we must work to make sure our words are always full of kindness, encouragement, and love.

Dear Father, controlling my tongue is hard to do. But I know I can do all things through Christ who gives me strength. Help me edit my words before they leave my mouth. Amen.

GOD'S FRIEND

It happened as the Holy Writings said it would happen. They say, "Abraham put his trust in God and he became right with God." He was called the friend of God.

JAMES 2:23

It's common to hear people talk about being God's child. But have you ever thought about how it might feel to be God's friend? A friend is someone we like and trust, someone we want to be around. A friend is someone we feel safe with because we know they won't betray us.

Abraham trusted God. He did what God told him to even when he didn't understand. Abraham's actions showed God that He could trust Abraham to do the right thing. We can be God's friends too. When we trust God, obey Him even when we don't understand, and spend time with Him because we want to, He calls us His friends as well.

Dear Father, I want to be Your friend. Like Abraham, I want to obey You even when I don't understand what You're doing. I want to spend time with You every day. I love You. Amen.

SUMMARY

Dear friends, let us love each other, because love comes from God. Those who love are God's children and they know God. Those who do not love do not know God because God is love.

1 John 4:7–8

In school we often have to give summaries. A summary tells the main points of a book, article, or movie. In these verses, John—who was Jesus' closest disciple—gives us a summary of God's Word. God is love, and as His children, we should also be love.

When people look at us, they should see the family resemblance. They should see so much love pouring out of our lives that they see God. John even says that if we don't love, we don't know God. If God is in us, His love will flow from us. The closer we are to Him, the more time we spend talking to Him and reading His Word, and the more like Him we become. The more like God we become, the more loving we are. How can you show God to the people around you? Love them.

Dear Father, I want to be love as You are love. Please make me like You. Amen.

SCRIPTURE INDEX

OLD TESTAMENT

NEW TESTAMENT

MORE GREAT BOOKS FOR STRONG GIRLS!

100 Extraordinary Stories for Courageous Girls

Girls are world changers! And this deeply inspiring storybook proves it! This collection of 100 extraordinary stories of women of faith—from the Bible, history, and today—will empower you to know and understand how women have made a difference in the world and how much smaller our faith (and the biblical record) would be without them.

Paperback / 978-1-63609-998-9

The Bible for Courageous Girls

Part of the exciting Courageous Girls series, this Bible provides complete Old and New Testament text in the easy-reading New Life™ Version, plus insert pages featuring full-color illustrations of bold, brave women such as Abigail, Deborah, Esther, Mary Magdalene, and Mary, mother of Jesus.

DiCarta / 978-1-64352-069-8

Find This and More from Barbour Publishing at Your Favorite Bookstore or www.barbourbooks.com